Woodturning:
an individual approach

Woodturning:
an individual approach

GUILD OF MASTER CRAFTSMAN PUBLICATIONS LTD

First published 2000 by
Guild of Master Craftsman Publications Ltd,
166 High Street, Lewes,
East Sussex, BN7 1XU

© GMC Publications 2000

ISBN 1 86108 160 X

Front cover photograph by Anthony Bailey,
Guild of Master Craftsman Publications Ltd.

Author photograph by kind permission of Alan Richards.

Other photography by kind permission of Dave Regester and the
Guild of Master Craftsman Publications Ltd.

A catalogue record of this book is available from the British Library.

Designed by Edward Le Froy.

Printed and bound by Kyodo Printing (Singapore) under the
supervision of MRM Graphics, Winslow, Buckinghamshire, UK

Contents

Health and Safety

Woodworkers must be aware of the potential dangers of their craft. The following guidelines offer what I consider to be the basic health and safety requirements for undertaking projects in this book.

Clothing and Eye Protection
- Wear strong shoes to protect the feet against dropped tools.
- Avoid wearing baggy, fussy clothes which may catch in the lathe.
- To protect the eyes at all times, wear either goggles, spectacles or a visor. An airstream helmet offers the best protection.

Dust control
Wood dust can cause serious health problems. It is also flammable and can explode. To protect against inhalation, use a dust mask and/or an extractor unit.

Electrics
Ensure that all machinery is properly earthed and installed. If in doubt, have it checked by a qualified electrician.

Fatigue
- Maintain a comfortable working height to reduce the risk of back strain.
- Always stop work if you are tired or unable to concentrate.

Grindstones
- Use a purpose-built grindstone that is properly enclosed and running at the correct speed.
- Check periodically the soundness of the stone.

Lathes
- Ensure that the lathe is bolted down and that the fixings are secure.
- Before switching on the power, ensure that all locking handles are tight, and revolve the work by hand to ensure that it spins freely and nothing catches.
- Always stand to one side when starting the lathe to avoid chips.
- Always turn off the lathe from the mains when loading or unloading, changing drive belts, or revolving the work by hand.
- Keep hands away from revolving chucks.
- Minimize the downward leverage on the tools by keeping the rest close to the workpiece; always reposition the rest rather than over-extend the tool.
- Remove the toolrest when sanding, and sand in the 'safe' position whenever possible.
- Discard timber which may come apart on the lathe, and beware of faults in the wood.

Lighting
Always ensure that your work area is well lit.

Turning tool use
- Keep tools sharp; a blunt tool is harder to control.
- The tool should be firmly supported by the toolrest before it touches the wood, and remain so while in contact with it.
- Always cut at a downward angle or with the grain.
- Scrapers should be kept flat on the toolrest and presented in the 'trailing' mode, with the handle higher than the tool edge.

Introduction

This book was inspired by the many kind and encouraging comments I have received from readers of my series of articles in *Woodturning* magazine. Its purpose is to consolidate my personal approach to woodturning and teaching woodturning, emphasizing the context of the workshop in this process.

Of course, every approach to this craft is a personal one, and each is equally valid. But I have found that my methods have been very successful with students and readers alike, and hope that they also benefit the beginner, for whom this book is primarily, but not exclusively, aimed. I firmly believe that the beginner learns more effectively by following a tutor's example closely, concentrating on how to manipulate a small, but comprehensive, range of tools. Once the beginner has a thorough grasp of the fundamentals, he or she can experiment with other methods and techniques to see if they suit better.

As the reader works through the projects, he or she will find that specific techniques are repeated. This is because many of the projects follow a similar method, but I believe repetition is a great help to the beginner – it is often not possible to remember everything you are told first time round. As a teacher I have learnt to repeat everything I say and it often proves invaluable.

Finally, whether you are a beginner or a craftsperson with a more advanced degree of proficiency, I am confident you will gain something of value from this book – from helpful hints and tips on how to create beautifully turned objects to a complete foundation in woodturning.

Dave Regester

TOOL TRUTHS

The basic tool kit

When I started turning in the early seventies it was hard to find specialist shops for turning tools and difficult to know which tools to use for which turning operation, never mind how to use or sharpen them.

Today, tools are easy to find and there is much more information about them. The problem is whose method do beginners adopt and which of the bewildering aray of tools do they choose?

The solution is to learn to use a few tools properly before you buy any more. This knowledge is best learnt from a good professional, who will usually recommend a basic tool kit consisting of maybe six tools, which is all you really need.

This minimises your outlay. You may also have to budget for a lathe,

Fig 1

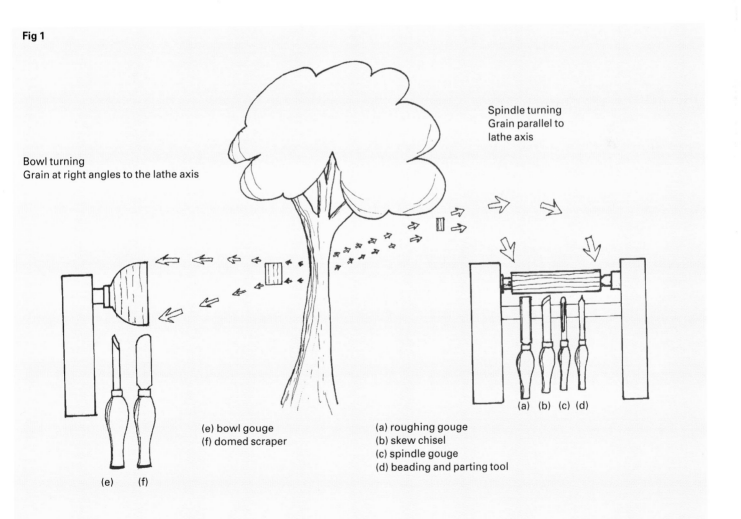

Bowl turning
Grain at right angles to the lathe axis

Spindle turning
Grain parallel to
lathe axis

(e) bowl gouge
(f) domed scraper

(a) roughing gouge
(b) skew chisel
(c) spindle gouge
(d) beading and parting tool

bench grinder and wood. When you have learned one method thoroughly you will be in a position to try others and different tools.

In this series I'll go into detail about each tool in turn, but will start by describing a basic set and making observations about tools in general.

It will help to prevent confusion as to the uses of the tools if you bear in mind that they are designed for either spindle turning or bowl turning. It's best not to challenge this basic concept until you've mastered the uses for which they are designed.

The important differences between the two uses are that in spindle turning the grain of the wood runs parallel with the axis of the lathe and the work is usually supported between two centres.

Grain

In bowl turning the grain of the wood is at right angles to the axis of the lathe and the work is supported on one face during each operation (Fig 1).

There is another type of turning – when you hollow into the end grain for objects such as boxes. The grain then runs parallel to the lathe's axis.

The work is supported at one end only, in a chuck, but the tools used to hollow the middle of a traditional bowl are not effective because of the grain direction.

So for hollowing end grain the tools used are the same as those used for spindles, with the addition of scrapers.

The basic tool kit I recommend (see photo) consists of: roughing gouge, skew chisel, spindle gouge, beading and parting tool, bowl gouge and domed scraper.

I have not specified tool sizes because it largely depends on the size of your budget. In the case of the roughing gouge, the bigger the better, but to save money you can buy a 19mm, ¾in to start with, as this is up to £20 cheaper than the 37mm, 1½in.

I use a 19mm, ¾in skew for most jobs, but a 25mm, 1in is preferred by some and only costs a couple of pounds more.

I have several sizes of spindle gouge in regular use but a 9mm, ⅜in is the one I use most. My beading and parting tool is 9mm, ⅜in.

Go for a medium-sized bowl gouge with a deep flute, either a 9mm, ⅜in or a 12mm, ½in. A half-domed scraper can be 19mm, ¾in, but a 37mm, 1½in is more stable inside a bowl, albeit a third more expensive.

Turning tool

A turning tool comprises the sharp end which does the cutting and a handle (see Fig 2). The junction between the two is achieved by a long tang on the blunt end of the metal bit which sticks into the handle.

This has to be long because of the leverage exerted at this point and the part of the handle where this takes place is strengthened by means of a ferrule, which is just a bit of metal tubing.

Tool makers supply handles for their tools, but many turners make their own. This is partly to suit their own habits and hand size, but also because it's easier to identify tools with different shaped ends when the

'Factory-made handles don't vary much from tool to tool. I find them acceptable, apart from the shiny varnish.'

business end is hidden by shavings.

Beginners should buy the basic kit already handled so they can practise turning before starting to make a finished object. But for more experienced turners, making a handle is easy.

The timber used is not critical, but ash has the right balance of lightness and strength. As to the shape and length of the handle, you'll find spindle tools are easier to use with quite short handles so they can pass in front of your body.

Longer handles are helpful for the

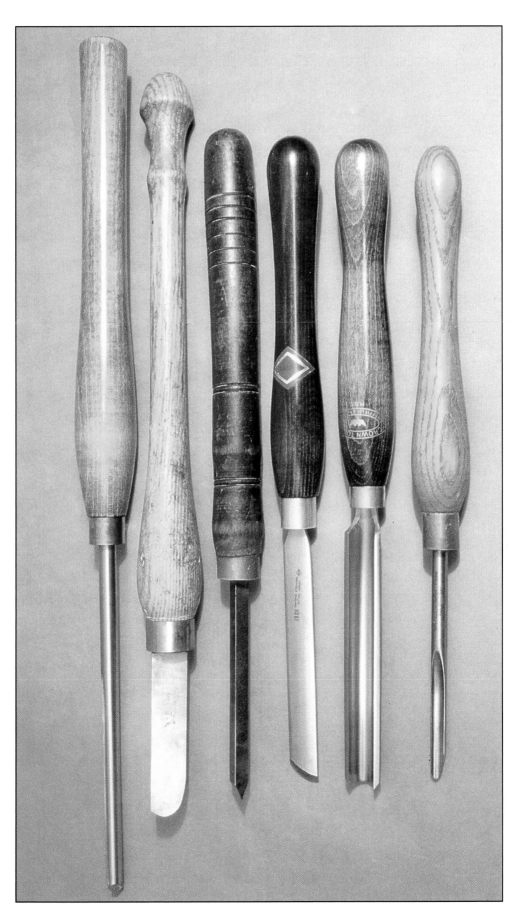

*A basic tool set
for beginners.*

larger bowl gouges, where they counterbalance the long overhang that can occur in a deep bowl.

Ferrules can be bought, but I use copper plumbing pipe.

Factory-made handles don't vary much from tool to tool. I find them acceptable, apart from the shiny varnish. This may look nice, but makes handles difficult to grip, especially when your hands are covered with finishing oil.

First thing

The first thing I do with a bought handle is to rub it with a bit of 60 grit abrasive. I never sand my home-made handles.

The metal used for turning tools needs to be hard enough to hold an edge when cutting hard timber at fast speeds, yet not so hard that it cannot be easily sharpened.

It has to be stiff enough to resist flexing between the tool tip and the rest, but not so stiff that it breaks under the strain.

sharp for up to six times longer, so need replacing less often. You spend less time sharpening and lose your temper less often.

Today, some manufacturers only supply high speed steel tools. Tools are still available in carbon steel from other manufacturers, but you may not be able to get the newer types of tool in this material.

The tools are usually made by outside contractors to the design of each supplier out of M2 stock and don't vary much in quality.

There are some slight differences in design and finish on standard tools that are largely a matter of personal taste, and the handles are made to different designs and out of different timbers.

Gouges are either ground out of round bar or forged from flat bar. Forged tools are more expensive and are supposed to be stronger, but that's - debatable.

They are made by beating metal into shape and, although this is a

much helpful advice. The one piece I can offer is that you bear in mind the characteristics required of a turning tool.

If you decide to convert an existing tool, such as a file, you will need to alter its temper, or it will snap when you put some leverage on it. And bear in mind where the shards of metal may fly!

There are six main tool suppliers in England. They are (in alphabetical order): Ashley Iles, Crown Tools, Home of Woodworking, Record, Robert Sorby and Henry Taylor. Tools are obtainable through hardware stores, some of which also supply them by mail order, such as Axminster Power Tools, John Boddy, Peter Child and Craft Supplies, whose catalogues are a valuable sources of information. I've found some variation between manufacturers in the length of useful steel. This can affect the balance of the tool but you may be surprised to hear that tools always get shorter in use anyway,

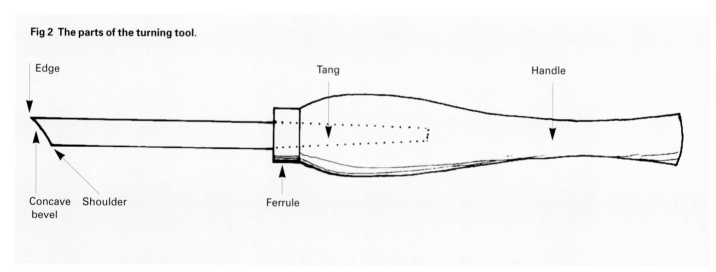

Fig 2 The parts of the turning tool.

Edge

Tang

Handle

Concave bevel   Shoulder

Ferrule

Before the flood, you could only get carbon steel tools and these were thought to be satisfactory for most purposes. Harder steels was too expensive for mere turning tools.

Eventually, high speed steel tools came onto the market. Tools made from this were more expensive than carbon steel, yet were soon taken up by professional turners.

Their advantage is that they stay

skilled job, the beating must affect the steel's molecular structure.

The most important difference between the two is the shape, particularly that of the spindle gouge. The forged tool is easier to grind to a fingernail shape. But it's largely a matter of what you are used to.

Competent metal workers may be tempted to make their own tools, but not being a metallurgist I can't offer

so the balance factor isn't really relevant.

What does matter is that longer tools last longer, so an initial saving might be a false economy if the tool is short.

None of the manufacturers mention tool length in their catalogues, which is to be expected if they vary, so if this worries you, take a tape-measure to a well-stocked store. ■

The vital area of sharpening

Choosing a benchgrinder

A grinding dream team. High speed grinder with Mick O'Donnell sharpening jig, on a stand to bring it to eye level. On the bench is a Tormek grinder fitted with a fingernail grinding jig.

I stressed in my last article that you should budget for a benchgrinder in your initial outlay. This is because it's vital your tools are sharp, or they won't cut wood, which is what turning is all about.

It's dangerous to 'save' money by cobbling together a home-made grinder. The grinding wheel must be guarded to catch the pieces should it disintegrate, and there should be a transparent flap over the edge of the wheel to stop sparks flying in your eyes should you have forgotten to wear eye protection.

The same safety considerations apply to putting a grinding wheel on the lathe. Since you must stop turning to fit it, it will disrupt your creative flow.

Selecting

When selecting a benchgrinder, choose one with wheels as wide as you can afford. But check also how soon it gets up to speed. Having decided to sharpen a tool, it's frustrating to wait for the grinder to wind itself up.

For similar reasons, the grinder should be placed close to the lathe.

So I don't have to bend when sharpening, I've made a stand that raises my grinder to eye level (see photo). This also makes it easier to view the tool from the side, to see the position of the bevel in relation to the stone's circumference.

Most high speed benchgrinders have two wheels. For high speed steel I recommend white aluminium oxide grind wheels, which also work for high carbon steel.

It's useful to have a coarse wheel (60 grit) for altering edge shapes and for remedial work, with a finer one for sharpening.

I use a 100 grit wheel, which gives an excellent edge to a tool, but this is soft and can lead inexperienced turners to apply too much pressure to the tool, causing blueing, which indicates a drawing of the temper.

Better option

When this happens, the tool will blunt quickly and you will need to grind it beyond the blue part. A better option for the beginner is to use an 80 grit stone for finer sharpening, or the Peter Child Pink Wheel, which is a blend of 80 and 100 grit.

This removes material quickly and gives a better edge than 60 grit, though not quite as fine as 100 grit.It does not blue the tool as readily as the latter can if you are heavy-handed.

Water-cooled grinders such as the Tormek are safer than benchgrinders because they grind slowly, and this excludes any possibility of drawing the temper.

But they are much more expensive than benchgrinders because of the speed reduction mechanism, and the slowness can deter those used to a bog standard grinder, which rotates fast.

I've found the edge obtained with the Tormek to be sharper than that obtained with a benchgrinder, and because it lasts longer it saves time in the long run.

Honed edge

Many turners use the tool straight from the grinder, on the basis that a honed edge, while sharper, does not retain its extra sharpness when pressed against a rotating piece of wood.

This is certainly true of gouges, but skew chisels cut cleaner when honed. If you don't have a honing wheel as on the Tormek, diamond whetstones are next best. Be sure to lubricate

them in the way the maker recommends, as this greatly enhances their efficacy and lengthens their life.

The bevel is the part of the tool ground away every time you sharpen a tool. When the tool's profile is correct and the bevel is right, the tool will cut properly.

The three factors that make for a good bevel are: one, concavity (hollow ground); two, a single facet; and three, the appropriate angle. The profile varies from tool to tool, so I'll discuss this when I deal with individual tools.

Concavity is achieved by sharpening against the outside of the wheel

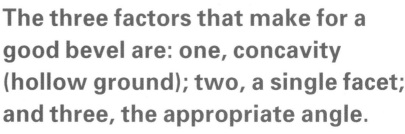

The three factors that make for a good bevel are: one, concavity (hollow ground); two, a single facet; and three, the appropriate angle.

and exactly matches the wheel's circumference.

It's a good thing for two reasons. First, because it enables the bevel to rub on the work when cutting, so supporting the tool and preventing dig-ins. Second, the edge lasts longer, for as it wears down the remaining metal is not as thick as it is with a flat or convex grind (Fig 1).

With single-facet grinding you should start at the shoulder and work up to the edge. In this way the edge is subjected for as short a time as possible to the heat generated by grinding. Because it is the tool's thinnest part, it heats up very quickly.

It's easy to see which part of the tool you are sharpening with a benchgrinder, since the sparks go between the edge and the stone when you sharpen near the shoulder. Only at the edge do they fly down over it and

along the top of the tool.

With a water grinder, this can be seen by viewing the wheel from the side. If you are in any doubt the bevel can be marked with a felt tip pen before you start and during the process you can take the tool away from the stone to see from where you've removed material.

Smoothly

If you move smoothly from the shoulder to the edge, you make only one facet on the bevel which will reflect the wheel's circumference. Then you will know the bevel is concave.

The third factor which makes for a good bevel is the appropriate angle. If all the wood you turned were to have a perfectly even texture, in other words if the molecules were evenly spread, then you could arrive at a mathematically ideal angle for the

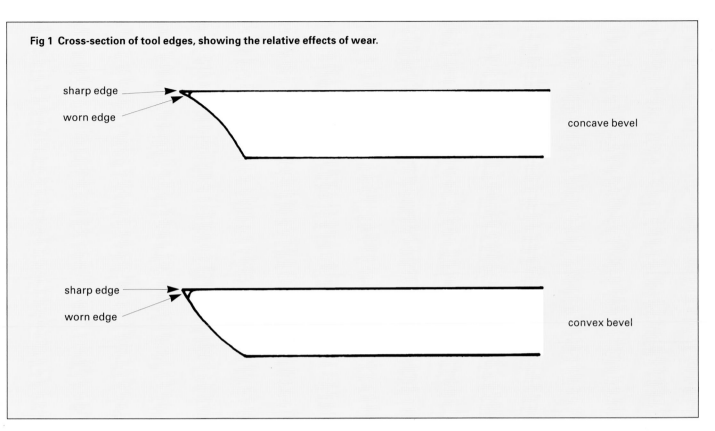

Fig 1 Cross-section of tool edges, showing the relative effects of wear.

sharp edge

worn edge

concave bevel

sharp edge

worn edge

convex bevel

cutting tool. Fortunately wood does not, so you cannot.

Within each piece of wood there are soft and hard bits and between species there is an even greater range.

It's not advisable, therefore, to say of any given tool that it should be ground at such and such an angle.

I never measured the angle of any of my bevels before I started to write about turning – if they worked I kept the angle the same and if they didn't I changed the angle until it did.

This is not particularly helpful to the beginner, so as a rough guide I suggest you adopt the angles shown below between the bevel and the tool body.

It's one thing to know what angle to aim for, quite another to achieve it. A professional learns through many hours of practice and sooner or later can reproduce a consistent angle-free hand.

The beginner can circumvent this learning process by buying a jig.

The best for benchgrinders is the Mick O'Donnell grinding jig and for Tormek grinders I recommend the fingernail jig and the table jig.

Both enable the tyro to get consistent bevel angles with the expenditure of some cash and time in setting them up.

It's one thing to know what angle to aim for, quite another to achieve it. A professional learns through many hours of practise

Roughing gouge 45°.

Skew chisel 30°.

Spindle gouge 30°.

Beading and parting tool 45°.

Bowl gouge 45°.

Domed scraper 45-50°.

You can tell when a good edge has been achieved by rubbing the edge against the ball of your thumb and seeing how quickly the blood flows.

Or, you can do the sensible thing and look at the edge in the light. If it flashes brightly, this is the bluntness reflecting light and you still have some way to go. If there's no reflection, you have what you want – an edge of minimal thickness. ∎

ROUGH STUFF

The roughing gouge and how to make a mallet

The roughing gouge is used to take the square edges off spindle blanks and to remove large amounts of wood in early shaping.

A deep flute gives this gouge its distinctive 'U' shape, designed to keep the corners out of contact with the timber. It comes in widths ranging from Ashley Isles' 9mm, ¾ in to Henry Taylor's 38mm, 1 ½ in.

The roughing gouge differs from the bowl gouge in having thinner steel in section, relative to its width, and a uniform thickness throughout the curve.

The larger roughing gouges narrow to a tang where the tool enters the handle, whereas most bowl gouges are ground from round stock and the part that fits in the handle is the same diameter as the rest of the tool.

Bowl gouges are thicker in section to make them more rigid when they are projected over the toolrest deep into a bowl. That's why roughing gouges should not be used for bowls.

Weak edges

I keep the bevel on my roughing gouge fairly short, about 45° because a long bevel makes for a weak edge. I use the tool strictly for the rough stuff.

You can get a good finish from the tool if it's nice and sharp, as you can see from the project. But my method is to get a rough shape with the gouge and do the rest of the work with a skew. This means the gouge does not have to be kept razor sharp, but the skew does.

All roughing gouges, except those made by Peter Child, have a straight-across profile, which works well. (Photo 2).

At times, I've sharpened more at the snout than on the wings, so eventually the snout becomes shorter than the wings. In other words, the tool develops horns.

This must be avoided like the Devil, because those horns can produce a nasty

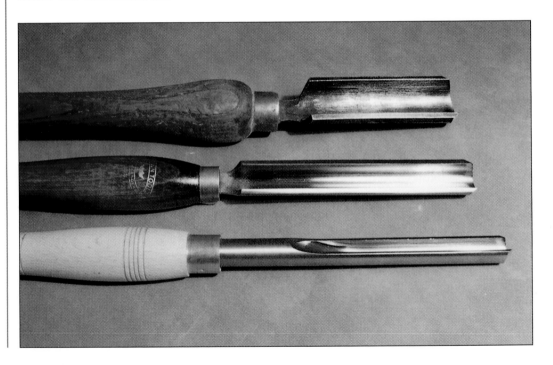

Three roughing gouges. Top, Sorby's 32mm, 1 ¼ in. Middle, Crown's 19mm, ¾ in. Bottom, Ashley Isles' 12mm, ½ in.

Bowl gouges are thicker in section to make them more rigid when they are projected over the toolrest deep into a bowl. That's why roughing gouges should not be used for bowls.

Photo 4 Grinding the bevel
on the ground back gouge.
Start with the right wing of a
gouge...

Photo 2 The profile of Ashley
Isles' 12mm, ½in roughing
gouge is straight across.

Photo 3 Changing the profile
from straight across to ground
back. Flats produced on the
corners are ground back until
the tip is reached.

catch. I now sharpen so that the snout sticks out, though not as far as it does in Peter Child's roughing gouge. This makes the tool more versatile and safe.

The straight-across roughing gouge is one of the easier tools to sharpen. If you have a sharpening jig such as the O'Donnell, you simply set the angle to 45° and rotate the tool from wing to wing so the edge is horizontal at all times.

If you start at the right-hand wing with your wrist fully rotated in the clockwise direction and keep your grip as you rotate the tool, it should be easy to keep a steady progress along the edge.

When using a bench grinder, a light touch is essential to avoid over-heating the edge. The sparks tell you both where on the edge you are sharpening and where on the bevel.

If the sparks disappear behind the edge, you are not sharpening all of the bevel, ie you have not yet reached the edge.

When using a whetstone like the Tormek, the harder you press the better (without stalling the motor), but you have no sparks by which to monitor progress.

If you don't have a jig on the benchgrinder, you will have to develop the knack of lining up the edge with some fixed point either on the grinder or on the wall behind, so you can be sure you are forming a single, consistent bevel, working from shoulder to edge.

You should be able to see if the angle of grind is correct from the look of the bevel, but if you find this difficult, try colouring the bevel with a felt tip before grinding.

'Feel' the bevel

Eventually, you will be able to monitor progress by the feel of the bevel on the stone. It just takes practice, ie years of turning full time, plus lots of tool steel and replacement stones.

To change the tool's profile from straight-across to ground-back, put the tool on its side on a flat rest, with both wings in contact with the circumference of the stone.

This produces flats on the edge (Photo 3) and when they meet at the snout you can then start to grind the bevel. It's not worth starting

on the bevel while there's a trace of the old profile showing as a semi-circle on the snout.

The ground-back profile is not as easy to sharpen as the straight-across. The tool handle has to swing across to keep the edge parallel to the grinder's axis to give a consistently concave bevel (Photos 4, 5 and 6).

Make a mallet

The first project I give students is to make a carver's mallet from a single lump of wood. But if you are an absolute beginner I suggest you attend a course before attempting this (or any other project) on the lathe. A good teacher will help with things I can't cover here, especially safety.

A good book or a video is only second best, because most students need the hands-on approach to support the theory.

The mallet is a good starting point because the shape is simple, but there is still scope for some design considerations and artistry.

Ideally, use a piece of unseasoned branch, as this is

less challenging, having no sharp corners to knock off and the greenness making it easier to cut.

As it should have cost you nothing, you can afford to make mistakes. And if you do complete it, with luck it will survive without cracking.

Otherwise, use any hardwood. I find a useful blank size is between 75mm, and 100mm, 3in to 4in diameter, and about 225mm, 9in long, with the grain running along the longer dimension.

I have used ash, sycamore, elm, oak, laburnum and black locust in the past, and have found the heavier the wood the better.

I regard these mallets as replaceable items because the wood is so cheap and they can be made in under 10 minutes, with practice.

If you have to use square-section stock you can make the job easier by removing the blank's corners with a plane. Then mount the blank between centres and set the lathe speed at slow, increasing it when you have a cylinder.

Roughing gouges are an excellent way of learning the basic techniques of gouge use. They are:

❶ Don't cut on the nose of the gouge, but just to the side (Photo 7). Choose the side nearest the support of the toolrest, ie the bottom side.

❷ The flute should point in the direction of the cut.

❸ Rub the bevel first and raise the tool handle slightly so that the edge begins to cut and immediately move the tool forward.

❹ Once the tool starts to cut, keep it at that angle as you move it across the workface. This means the end of the

Photo 5 (above left) ...sweep round to the snout, and...

Photo 6 (above right) ...continue on to the left wing.

Photo 7 The roughing gouge is used on its side, the flue towards the direction of traverse.

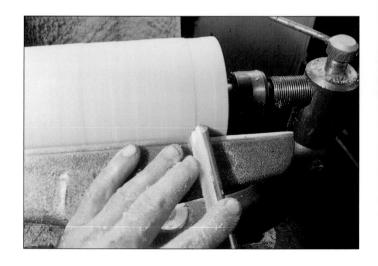

Photo 8 Heavy cuts for the handle of the mallet.

Photo 9 Checking the mallet handle for size.

handle should move at the same rate as the cutting end is moving across the toolrest. It's best achieved by supporting the tool with the body and then moving the body by switching the weight from one foot to another. Just using the arms is not as steady.

For your first gouge cut it's best to use a rounded blank, such as a branch or an old chair leg. Then you can work out the angle to hold the tool so that the bevel supports the edge and you reduce the number of dig-ins.

When confronted with a whirring square section blank, you have to look upon the outside edges as your target to set the tool angle, not the solid lump within.

It will seem awesome at first, but with a firm grip and face protection, you will find it quite exciting to reduce a rough blank to a cylinder with just a few passes of the tool.

I move the gouge from right to left and then left to right, but some prefer to work in one direction only, towards the tailstock, with heavy cuts. I don't think there's much to choose between the two in terms of speed.

You can tell when the blank is round by resting the back of the tool on the rotating work. When there are no more vibrations, you're there.

The toolrest will now have to be moved in closer and, with the lathe stopped, you can inspect the blank for defects. These may have to be taken into account when deciding which end will be the handle.

Turn spigots

The next stage is to turn spigots at both ends to give a margin of error, in case the tool slips towards the centres. They will also enable you to part off the work, leaving no traces of holes left by the centres.

This calls for a steep cut at right angles to the lathe's axis. This is not easy with a gouge, because it has to be lined up precisely, with the bevel at right angles to the axis to keep control.

It's easier to develop a round shoulder by making the roughing cut heavier where the spigot will be and, when the cut is finished, going back to where the shoulder will start.

You line up the gouge in

the position you were roughing out with the bevel rubbing but the edge not in contact and then twist the gouge to start cutting.

As you move the tool along the cut, you keep twisting it so the cuts gets deeper. Aim for depth rather than sideways movement.

With spigots at both ends, the handle can be formed with heavy-duty cuts (Photo 8) and the junction between head and handle made as sharp as possible, so the hand can push right up against the head.

Adjust handles

The thickness of the handle can be adjusted to fit your hand, but try it out with the rest removed and the wood at rest (Photo 9).

A finishing cut can be made with the roughing gouge, but you will probably need to sharpen it. What makes for a good finish from the tool is the thinness of the cut which results from the closeness of the bevel support.

There should be no need to sand your mallet, as a smooth handle isn't easy to grip and the head is soon to suffer re-texturing in use.

I failed to mention this in one demonstration, and on my next visit was proudly shown a brilliantly finished and lovingly polished mallet which I was told was too good to be used.

Parting off can't be done with a gouge. But you can saw off the spigots while the mallet is still supported between centres, or just wait for my next thrilling instalment on parting tools. ■

BEADING AND PARTING

The beading and parting tool is a straight chisel made from 9mm, ¹¹⁄₃₂ in square section steel. It has two bevels 30-45°, square across the end and can be used for several purposes.

I use it for removing bulk at the ends of spindles to create spigots and for turning deep, square-sided grooves larger than 9mm wide. It can also be used to turn beads.

The most efficient way to use the tool to remove wood at right angles to the axis of the lathe is shown in the diagram over the page. The rest should be level with the centre of the axis or slightly higher, depending on your height and how high you have the lathe.

If you hold the tool so the edge is away from the wood but the bevel rubbing and then raise the end of the handle, the edge will come into contact and will start cutting.

If you don't know how the tool works you can try this

There are rough edges to a beading and parting tool cut.

Making a groove.

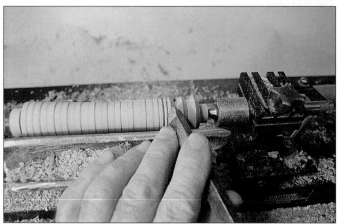

with the motor off and rotate the wood by hand. But it's quite safe to do it with the lathe running.

As soon as the edge bites into the wood the tool must be pushed over the rest and down towards the centre, so that if you were to continue, the edge would pass through the centre, at which point it would be below the level of the rest.

Needless to say, only go this far if you want to part the wood! The tool will feel as though it's about to snatch if you do this correctly, but you must be firm and keep the tool moving.

As you gain in confidence you will find you can remove wood quickly with this method. But the beading and parting tool tends to leave the edges of the groove rough and if these need to be cleaned up, a further cut with the tool on its side will be necessary.

You should avoid pushing the tool horizontally into the wood. It may feel less hazardous, but it does not cut as quickly and the edge soon blunts. You produce dust instead of shavings and the surface at the bottom of the groove won't have a good finish.

Spigots

The purpose of spigots on the ends of the work is partly so holes produced by the centres can be avoided when parting, and they also serve as a safety gap, preventing mistakes from ending in accidental driving centre or tool modifications.

You need to take this into account by allowing extra when cutting the blank, and the length of this depends on how far the centres penetrate into the wood and how much wood you need to part off.

Professional turners like to part items such as honey dippers down to a fine point at either end, to minimise the finishing needed off the lathe.

The spigots can also be part of the object, such as, in the case of furniture, spindles which need to fit other parts.

In this case the centre holes probably disappear up the hole and can be ignored, but the spigots need to be sized and this can be done using callipers. These are quickly adjusted to the diameter you require, but tend to widen with use.

For repetition turning, a spanner of the right size is best, as the gap never alters. A collection of big, old spanners is invaluable and a good excuse to rummage in second-hand tool shops.

Beginners who hang onto the tool like grim death, with both hands, will need to stop the lathe to check the diameter of the spigot.

As they gain in skill, they'll find they can hold the tool in one hand and the callipers in the other, as shown in the photo. The tool is held firmly because the end of the handle is pressing against my thigh, my right hand is holding the handle and the tool is pressing down on the rest.

If spigot dimensions are critical, I set the callipers to slightly larger than the required size and remove a final sliver, checking with a Vernier gauge.

It's no good thinking you can take off that final little bit with abrasives, because the spigot won't remain round due to the variable hardness of different parts of the grain.

The spigot's length is often greater than the tool's width, in which case you need not measure every cut. You can usually judge the diameter of the rest of the spigot by eye or, if it's very long, do a

Starting to roll a bead.

The cut which finishes the bead.

The beading and parting tool pealing cut.

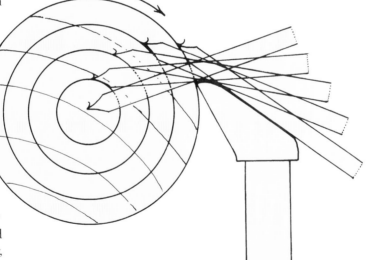

couple of sized cuts and join them up.

As always, it's good practice to master the tool on a piece of wet branchwood before attacking a piece of wood you have to pay for. Once roughed out with a roughing gouge, make spigots at both ends and roll some beads.

The first rule of bead rolling is that you start at the tip of the shoulder and

gradually extend the rounding process until you reach the fattest point, which usually needs just a thin smoothing cut. In other words, don't try and make the bead in one go.

Start at the right-hand end and, with the tool flat on the rest, get the bevel rubbing without the edge cutting. Raise the handle until the edge bites and roll the tool over to the right so that the right hand point of the edge makes a thin

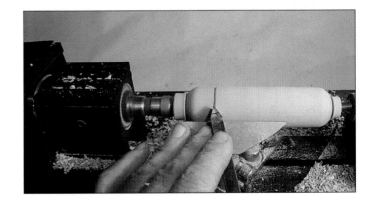

Marking the knob.

groove in the wood.

The handle end should be raised so the point has the support of the bevel as it moves around the bead. You get a smooth curve if you make that thin groove progress across the face of the bead in one flowing movement.

At the end of the cut the tool should be on its side, with the point at the bottom of the bead and the tool should be horizontal or with the cutting end lower than the handle end, depending on how high the rest is positioned.

Avoid catches

Catches can occur if part of the edge other than the point come into contact with the wood. This can be avoided by making sure that the handle end stays to the left of the point and the end is gradually raised as the tool is rolled.

Vee cuts are made by marking the centre of the groove with the tool on its side and using the bottom point. You then rotate the tool in a clockwise direction until the bottom bevel is aligned with the direction of

Fig 2 Bead cut in stages

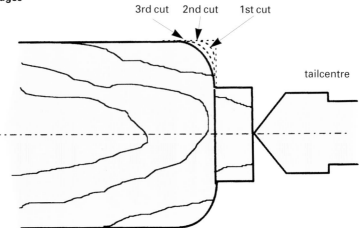

the right hand side of the intended vee.

The handle is then raised to the right so the point goes down and to the left into the wood, towards the centre of the intended vee.

The other side is done in the same way. All this means that the tool handle end is to the right of a line at right angles to the axis of the lathe when turning the right hand side of the vee, and to the left when turning the left-hand side.

Make a pestle

When beading and parting tool cuts have become second nature, you may like to try to make a pestle.

After roughing out and

making the end spigots, you will see what I mean about the sides of the cuts being quite rough. But that doesn't matter here, as both ends need to be rounded.

When this has been done,

The shaft in a series of strips.

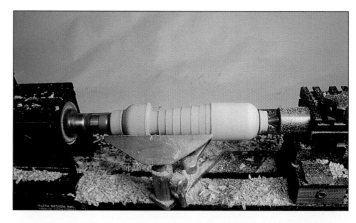

Starting the shaft.

Smoothing the shaft.

16 *Woodturning – an individual approach*

Smoothing the side.

The finish given by the beading and parting tool on the foot massager.

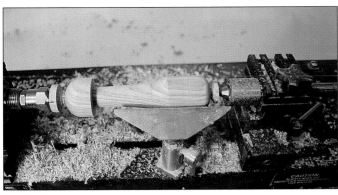

The finish from the tool.

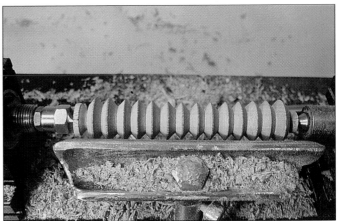

the position of the knob should be marked out with the tool on its side, so the fibres don't break out when the bulk of the shaft is removed.

The waste is shifted with the peeling cut down to the required thickness and another cut is made next to that one, but not so deep so that you end up with a series of steps, forming the required shape.

This is then smoothed, with the point of the edge moving from right to left (downhill) followed by a smoothing cut with the middle of the edge. I have used a fibre tip pen to mark the cutting part of the edge.

I once had to quote for making thousands of foot massagers for a well known shop but, strangely enough, could not compete with Eastern imports, for which I was grateful.

A foot massager is just a cylinder of any hardwood (a splintery wood would not be a good idea) with a series of grooves on them. The idea is that you roll your foot over it and it allegedly does you good.

London plane

For the project I used a blank of London plane (*Platanus x hybrida*) about 37 x 37 x 150mm , approx 1 ½ x 1 ½ x 6in , which is roughed out and has spigots at both ends. The resultant available wood is about 135mm, 5¼in long. Mark the centre with a pencil while the work is rotating, and do a peeling cut there to reduce the diameter to about 25mm, 1in. Using a series of shallower and shallower cuts, make the stepped profile

needed and smooth it with the tool point so the profile is a shallow vee.

Mark the centre again and add more marks every 5mm, ³⁄₁₆in, alternating thick and thin. These will be the peaks and troughs of the vees which are made as I've described.

When you can get even vees with no ornamental spirals on the peaks, give yourself a pat on the back. ∎

Sizing with callipers.

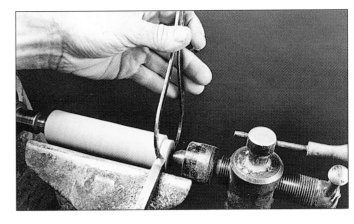

Spindle gouges

Spindle gouges come in a wide range of sizes, from micro up to 32mm, 1 ¼ins. Those up to about 13mm, ½in are mainly used for detailed work on spindles, but they are also useful for hollowing out end grain bowls.

Some turners choose the spindle gouge for beads and coves on balusters etc, and in skilled hands it is as good as a skew chisel for such features. The larger sizes can be used for turning less delicate features and roughing out.

The difference between spindle gouges and the two other main types of gouge (roughing and bowl) is that the flute is much shallower in the former.

To confuse matters, there are at least three types of spindle gouge. Tool sellers do not always supply all three, and the names they give them vary.

The Robert Sorby catalogue has the clearest scheme for separating the three, naming them Standard strength, Long and strong, and Continental type.

Standard strength gouges are like Long and strong in that the smaller sizes (up to 13mm, ½ in) are ground from solid, round bar, but the Standard strength has a deeper flute and consequently thinner section, which gives a longer edge with a shorter bevel when ground back. This makes it better for producing finer detail and is the style I prefer.

In the larger sizes, all styles are forged to shape from flat bars, producing a flatter curve. The difference between the Standard strength and the Long and strong is in the thickness of the section. The Continental

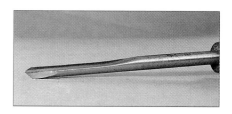

The tool is ground with a longer bevel on the left-hand side, because this is the side used for hollowing into end grain.

style differs from the others in that all sizes are forged from flat bars. It has a deeper flute and is flatter on the top of the edges of the flute.

Sorby grind the Continental with a 60° bevel and a more rounded profile. The 13mm, ½ and 19mm, ¾in are the most popular sizes and can be used both for roughing out

To round the right-hand end of the blank, hold the gouge so that the bevel is rubbing the work but the edge is not in contact...

...the tool should be on its side with the bevel pointing to the right and the handle well down.

The tool's position at the end of the cut. Notice how it is now well over to the right to keep the bevel close to the wood.

The same stage as shown left, the tool handle now higher than the rest. This cut is repeated until the end is rounded off.

The left-hand side of the cove is cut by rotating the wrist holding the handle clockwise at the start of the cut

and for planing cuts. The longer bevel enables you to achieve a much finer cut.

All well known tool companies make decent spindle gouges. The differences between them are mainly in blade length and steel thickness in the base of the flute.

The one you choose is chiefly a matter of personal preference and price. I go for the models which are thinner in section.

If you are inexperienced, make a 10mm, ⅜in Standard strength gouge part of your basic kit. This will enable you to practise basic spindle gouge techniques and to use it as an end grain hollowing tool.

If you subsequently master the skew chisel, you will still find uses for such a spindle gouge. But if the skew defeats you, invest in a larger spindle gouge to supplement the smaller one.

Sharpening

Apart from the Continental type, spindle gouges from most manufacturers are ground with a slight curve on the end. You can view this in two ways – as something which gives freedom to grind to the shape you prefer, or as something quite useless.

To use the tool to its full potential you need to grind it so that the bevel extends down the sides. This is done

in the same way as for the roughing gouge. First you change the profile by resting the tool upside down on the grinder's rest, in other words so that the flute is pointing down.

Then you grind both wings of the edge at once, leaving the nose unaltered.

Look at the tool with the flute pointing towards you and you will see the nose still has an edge but that the wings are flat. So you need to make bevels on either side of the tool which blend in with the bevel remaining on the nose.

This is done by holding the tool at the grinder so that the bottom of the tool is on the toolrest with the flute pointing up and the flats you have just made are horizontal.

Visualise making a bevel on the side of the tool to meet up with the original bevel on the nose. You need to grind away the side of the tool up to and through the flat you formed, so it becomes an edge.

To start, grind a straight side bevel, and gradually add a curve to blend into the bevel at the nose. This entails bringing the handle round towards your body as you grind.

As with all grinding operations, you won't progress faster by pressing harder, as this simply blues the edge.

I grind on one side and then on the other, to avoid overheating. I grind the tool with a longer bevel on the left hand side, because this is the side I use for hollowing into end grain.

The best way to master any tool is by practising shapes over and over again on a cheap branch or offcut. There is then less tension, because you are not worried about the cost and you are not trying to replicate a shape for a project. It sounds boring but is, in fact, therapeutic.

I used a roughing gouge to rough out the 150 x 38 x 38mm, 6 x 1 ½ x 1 ½in piece of cedar shown on these pages. And a beading and parting tool to turn spigots on both ends, to remove the danger of contacting the driving and revolving centres with the gouge.

Develop skills

If you can master the beads and coves of spindle tuning, you will develop the skills needed to turn other shapes.

A bead is a round lump, long or short, and a cove is a hollow. You cannot make a bead without having some sort of hollow on either side, so making several of them is a good exercise.

Once you've roughed out the blank and got rid of the flats, start rounding at the shoulder of the bead by taking a thin sliver off the edge (cut 1a in the drawing over the page) and then a longer sliver (cut 2a), and so on. Don't touch the middle of the bead, except for a finishing cut at the end.

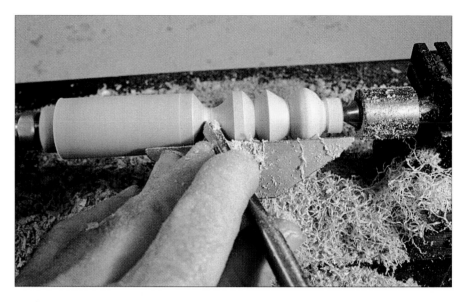

The toolrest should be set so that tool can cut to the centre of the work with the bevel supporting the edge. This means the rest should be level with, or just above, the centre depending on your height relative to the lathe. The flute should point in the direction of the cut.

Bevel rubbing

To round off the right-hand end of the blank, hold the gouge so that the bevel is rubbing the work but the edge is not in contact. The tool should be on its side with the bevel pointing to the right and the handle well down.

The edge is only about 5mm, ³⁄₁₆in from the end of the shoulder, and as you are cutting with the side of the tool, it will be a shearing cut.

To cut the wood, raise the hand

Rotate the wrist holding the handle anti-clockwise as you near the bottom, to reduce the amount of wood removed.

gently and rotate the wrist clockwise until the edge begins to bite.

Then move the tool to the right, continuing to rotate it and to raise the handle. The rate at which you do this is the difficult bit to master. The only answer is to keep trying until you get it right.

If you don't have a catch when doing this for the first time, you are probably not trying hard enough. Provided you are wearing protective gear, especially for the face, you should be safe.

A catch will probably make you jump, but it's part of the learning curve, so long as you can analyse where you went wrong.

Cutting the right-hand side of the cove is a mirror image of the left-hand operation – the tool rotates anti-clockwise at the start...

...then clockwise near the bottom.

At the bottom of the cove only a sliver should be removed and the cut should feather in to the other side, with no discernible ridge.

Try to keep the lathe in position at the end of the catch, so you can work back to where the dig-in occurred. Study the position of your hands and of the tool, and try to compare them to the photos shown here.

Catches usually result from the bevel being too far from the surface. If you find that you don't have catches but simply cease cutting before reaching the bottom of the cut, it means the bevel is rubbing but the edge is not in contact. The answer is to raise the tool handle more.

At the end of the cut, the tool should be well over to the right to keep the bevel close to the wood.

To make a cove to the left of the rounded end, make a shallow vee cut where the deepest point will be. This is done with the side of the gouge, as before, but because you should always cut so that the fibres being cut are supported by those beneath (downhill on a spindle), you should cut the left-hand side of the vee with the right-hand side of the gouge (cut 1 on the drawing) and then the right-hand side of the vee with the left-hand (cut 2 on drawing).

Correct angle

Take care to start the first few cuts with the bevel rubbing on the flat section of the blank and rotating the tool into the cut; a wrong angle of approach will result in a decorative but unintentional spiral executed by an out-of-control tool.

When you have had sufficient

practice, you will be able to present the tool at just the right angle to shear straight into the wood, but don't be in a hurry to get to that level of skill.

By widening and deepening each side of the vee in turn, you will eventually remove the bulk of the waste from the cove and can then produce the required concave sides by rolling the wrists as you decend.

The left-hand side of the cove is made by rotating the wrist holding the handle clockwise at the start of the cut, to take out more material, and then anti-clockwise near the bottom, to reduce the amount of wood removed. The operation is reversed for the right-hand side. Avoid cutting uphill on the other side of the cove, as this is cutting against the grain and will result in a rough finish at best and a catch at worst.

Depth of cut

The depth of cut is controlled by the distance between the work and the bevel. The experienced turner develops a feel for this, so that the amount of material removed results not from greater force but the amount of support from the bevel.

At the bottom of the cove, remove only a sliver of a shaving, and blend the cut into the one on the other side, with no discernible ridge.

These cuts can be done as easily by the skew chisel, but there's one situation where I've found a narrow spindle gouge the only tool for turning a cove – when a narrow cove is required next to a pommel (square sided section). This seems to be a favourite design feature, but there is no way you can get a skew chisel to cut the side of the cove adjacent to the pommel without catching the square corners.

I'll describe the use of the spindle gouge for hollowing end grain bowls in a later article, but if you can't wait the only crumb of comfort I can offer is covered in the book, *Turning Boxes and Spindles: Step by Step*, by one David Regester (published by Batsford). ■

7 5 3 1   2 4 6 8   3(a) 2(a) 1(a)

Sequence of cuts for beads and coves

The nightmare begins

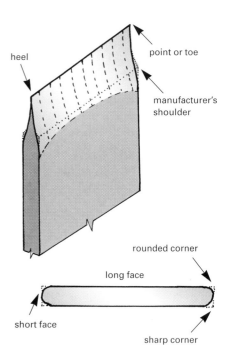

Beginner's nightmare: the skew chisel

Strange to say, a skew chisel is a chisel with an edge that is skewed! This means that the edge is not straight across the end of the tool but at an angle, usually 60°.

The skew was originally made from rectangular cross-section steel, but now comes in many shapes and sizes., which can confuse beginners.

If you don't already have a skew chisel, I suggest you start with an oval section 19mm, ¾in.

I've used many of the skews currently available and they all perform well when sharpened the way I like.

Versatile

The tool was developed for turning spindles and there is little you cannot do with a skew. Indeed it has so many uses, it will take more than one article to describe them.

While its versatility in spindle work is beyond doubt, it's not a tool the beginner should use on other sorts of work where the grain runs at 90° to the lathe axis (ie most bowl blanks).

For it's difficult to control when used on the rapid sequence of end and side grain that is repeated twice per rotation.

I have found that while some of my pupils learn to use it quite quickly, others struggle.

For those who don't grasp the principles quickly, practice is the only answer. You must turn every day, like a professional. After turning eight hours a day, six days a week, for several years, you should be getting there.

The three main types of skew chisel, defined by the cross section of the steel they are made from, are rectangular, oval and round.

The edge ground by manufacturers is usually straight and the angle of skew is about 60°. The end of the edge with the acute angle is called the point or toe, and the other end, the heel.

Many professionals now grind the edge with a curve. I was introduced to this by Richard Raffan, and at once found it easier to use.

Later, I developed some cuts with the curved skew that are not possible with a straight edge, such as turning narrow coves. It's a good tool for a beginner, being less likely to catch.

The curve I give my edges varies, so in my tool kit I keep a wide selection of profiles to choose from. As with so many things, you try different shapes and eventually find those that suit you best.

Rectangular

The rectangular skew is the traditional type, but it usually altered in two ways:
- The place where the bevel meets the stock (the shoulder) is often rounded at both ends, because a sharp shoulder can mark the work. This is more noticeable

Modifications to rectangular section skew.

with a skew than other tools, because it is often used with the bevel rubbing on the work, particularly for finishing cuts.
- The sharp corners of the tool stock are also radiused. If left sharp they tend to cut into the toolrest, which causes the tool to snag when traversing the rest. They also make it hard to produce a bead.

When rolling a bead the tool has to rotate from its long face onto its short face and if the corners are not rounded this makes it harder to control.

Oval

To incorporate these modifications into the tool, skew chisels were made from oval section stock. This gives

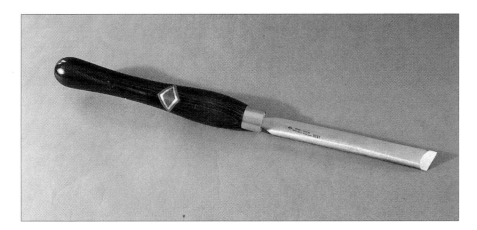

Henry Taylor's 19mm, ¾in oval skew, unsharpened.

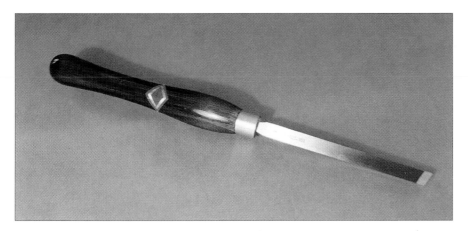

The 19mm, ¾in rectangular section skew from Henry Taylor, unsharpened.

the above advantages without secondary sharpening. They usually have radiused corners on the heel face, but flats on the point face.

Round

Modifying skews to a logical conclusion has produced a skew edge ground on the end of a round rod, circular in cross-section.

This tool slides over the rest as easily as an oval section skew, and can be easily rotated for rounding cuts.

But the traditional type is still first choice for many turners, because the above modifications make it stable on the toolrest and less prone to flexing than oval section skews.

I find a traditional skew essential when cutting a pommel. For the wood's square sections cause the tool to bounce and the extra rigidity and support of the flat, short face of the stock, enables a clean, straight cut to

be made where an oval section skew is thrown off course and leaves a ribbed face.

The round section skew has more bulk than the oval, and is not prone to flexing. I've heard that it's the easiest skew to learn, but I can't do all that I want with it – the extra bulk makes the tool unsuitable for narrow coves and getting under rings.

Sharpening

The straight-edged skew is fairly easy to sharpen, because as long as you can reproduce the bevel angle you simply slide the tool from side to side on the rest.

If you want to curve the edge, place the tool flat on the grinder rest with the tool pointing towards the centre of the wheel, and get the profile right before grinding the bevel.

This changed profile does not need to touch the point, which needs no

alteration. Indeed it should be left alone at this stage. A sharp point is essential to the way I use the tool.

If you grind away a sharp point you won't be able to do as much with the curved skew as you ought.

To grind the bevels on the curve, you have to move the edge through an arc on a pivot point on the tool-rest, so that each part of the edge is horizontal while it is being ground to maintain the same concavity along the bevel.

Important

It's important to keep both bevels the same length, so that when the tool is turned it feels the same and cuts at the same angle.

When sharpening an oval section skew, rock it slightly as the edge passes along the wheel. The easiest way to do this is to hold the tool between your body and the grinder, with your nose in line with the edge of the wheel when grinding both bevels.

This means you do not shift position when going from one side to the other and the edge's position to the wheel therefore looks the same.

When you are practised at sharpening, it's the feel of the bevel on the wheel that guides you. But until you

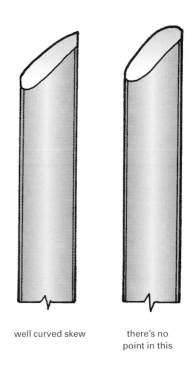

well curved skew   there's no point in this

Curved edge profiles – right and wrong.

reach that level, aim to keep the edge at the same height on the wheels's outer face by lining it up with a fixed point such as a mark on the grinder's casing.

A touch of felt-tip pen on the bevel will soon reveal which bit of the edge you are grinding.

The angle of the bevels should be about 15° between it and the shaft, ie. a profile angle of 30°. A longer bevel (smaller profile angle) gives a sharper edge, but is harder to control.

If you sharpen with a water-cooled grinder such as a Tormek, you will notice that the edge produced is much better than that produced on a bench-grinder. Also, that honing the edge on the leather wheel makes it even better.

This edge seems to last a long time, partly due to the coolness of the sharpening and because the fine stone produces such a smooth edge.

Support

I use the universal support for skew sharpening, but if you need more guidance, the flat-rest can be set at the angle wanted. You can even use the fingernail gouge jig invented by Tormek for sharpening an oval skew (see Test Report, Issue 38).

The skew has so many different uses that it's worth thinking of it as three separate tools – the plane, the slicer and the peeler.

Using it as a plane is the best way of making a straight or gently curved cylinder smooth. As a slicer it will cut so cleanly across endgrain that abrasives roughen the surface. As a peeler it can remove long shavings as fast as the beading and parting tool.

Either hand

I hold the tool in either hand at the rest, because it's easier to change hands than to move the body, and because the lathe sometimes gets in the way.

It's also easier to replicate shapes if you keep your head in the same position to the piece.

I hold the tool in an unusual way, with my little finger and the one next to it keeping contact with the rest and the second one on the bottom edge

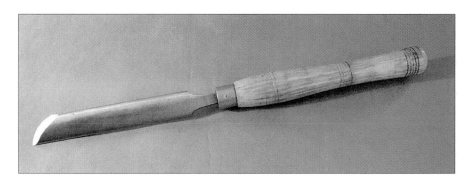

Ashley Iles' 25mm, 1in oval skew, sharpened.

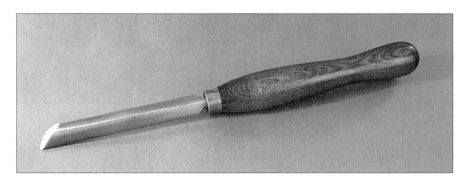

Crown Tools' 19mm, ¾in oval skew, sharpened.

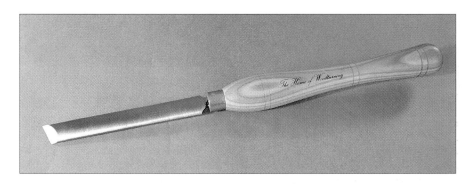

Home of Woodturning's 19mm, ¾in oval skew, unsharpened.

The author's unusual grip on the toolrest.

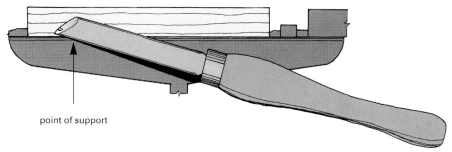

point of support

Good planing cut – toolrest close to the work and at the right height.

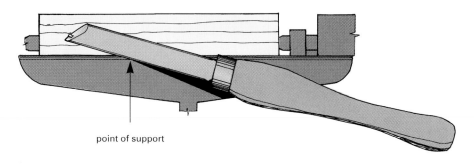

point of support

Poor planing cut – the toolrest close to the work, but too low, with support too far from the cutting edge.

of the tool. The first finger is on top. This has come about sub-consciously, but I've found my pupils gain more control when they try it.

Catches

Everyone who has ever used a skew chisel has had a catch, and many who use a skew are fearful of adding unintentional spiral details to their work.

You have a catch because you lose control of the tool. This occurs for two reasons:
- The bevel is not supporting the edge.
- The support from the rest is too far away from the part of the tool which is cutting.

To ensure the bevel nearly rubs the work, begin every edge cut (eg planing) by resting the bevel on the work with the edge not cutting and raise the handle (with the tool still on the rest) so that the edge bites.

Then, move the tool along the rest, keeping the same angle in relation to the lathe's axis. If the edge is lined up at about 45° to the axis, traverse along the work, keeping the tool at a constant angle.

The best way to do this is to move your body by shifting your weight from one foot to the other, rather than just moving your arms.

Supporting the bevel extends the life of the edge, because the edge is presented to the wood at the best angle to cut efficiently.

The thinnest cut for maximum quality of finish and a burnish from the bevel comes when it rubs the work. To remove material quickly, raise the bevel higher from the surface. Keep the tool moving and apply little force, or the tool will try to burrow into the wood and even split it.

Take it easy

Experience will tell you how far you can force a piece of wood. Until you gain this, you will progress fastest by taking it easy.

Lack of close support by the toolrest can be because the 'rest is not as close to the work as it could be, or because it is too low.

The toolrest can be close to the work but too low, and if it's angled like the Graduate rest, the point where it is supporting the tool may

not be the top edge but further down and a long way from the work.

If you have the bevel rubbing but are still finding it hard to control the skew, stop the lathe while keeping the tool's position on the rest and see if there is a big distance between the part on the rest and the part doing the cutting.

The point where the tool sits on the rest is the fulcrum between the edge and the hand on the handle. If the distance between the resting point and the edge is as small as possible, the hand movement on the handle becomes a small movement of the edge.

But if the distance between the resting point and the edge is fairly large , the hand movement on the handle is converted to a relatively large movement of the edge.

Margin for error

In other words, the nearer the resting point is to the edge, the greater the margin for error. A twitch of the hand on the handle is not converted to a potentially hazardous lurch of the edge.

Another problem of a long overhang is that the tool can flex between rest and work the very small amount that can cause snatches.

Next month, I'll describe the skew chisel's different functions, and discuss the advantages of the point-down rather than heel-down method, with a project. ■

Mastering the skew

Different functions and techniques

W atch a skew master at work and you'll see how shaping is done in a continuous flow, with planing, beads and coves merging. There seems to be no thought about each type of cut, nor about how it's done.

You can only reach this level of expertise by practising different ways of using the skew until its use becomes second nature.

There are three main kinds of cut: planing, slicing and peeling. The planing cut is used to make a cylinder or a gradual curve, smooth.

It will aid your understanding of the processes involved if you try the following exercise on a piece of stationary softwood, say 50 x 50 x 300mm, 2 x 2 x 6in, held in a vice.

Take any flat chisel, be it a skew or an ordinary, firmer chisel, and try to smooth the wood. You'll find you can do this by cutting along the grain with the bevel pressed lightly to the surface.

If the timber is not straight grained, the only way to get a smooth finish is to cut across the grain at an angle. This also applies to turning.

When you try it, you will see that the grain direction of the rotating spindle, while remaining in the same general orientation, changes subtly all the time.

Makes life easier

The spindle turner tries to make life easier by choosing straight-grained timber and cutting the blank with the grain running parallel to its long axis.

But this does not always succeed. Occasionally, a twisted bit of grain will appear which will be hard to smooth with the skew. You need develop your skills to overcome this by slightly changing the angle of the tool. If your knuckles are white with worrying about small catches, you

will be too tense to be delicate with your adjustments.

Before you practice a planing cut, you need to make the blank round with a spindle roughing gouge. Before attacking it with the skew, it's a good idea to stop the lathe and hold the tool with the edge at 45° to the axis and the bevel flat on the wood.

If you rotate the wood towards you by hand, you can produce a small shaving by raising the

Planing cut with a firmer chisel, the bevel rubbing

handle. This shows you the angle to hold the tool, then you can try the same operation with the lathe providing the power.

I start a planing cut with the edge at 45° to the axis, but alter the angle according to how the wood is responding, so it's usually at a smaller angle, like that shown in the photo at the bottom of page 64.

You will see that the part of the edge doing the cutting is next to the point. The great thing about having a curved edge is that if the grain is so twisted that you cannot get a good finish

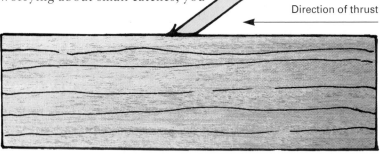

Direction of thrust

Planing cut, using the point of an oval section skew.

from the tool, you can try a cut with the edge more or less parallel to the axis.

With a curved edge, only a small part of the edge is in contact, so it's easy to control. With a straight-edged skew the whole of the edge is in contact and both points want to dig in at once.

Look carefully while the bevel is rubbing without the edge cutting and you should be able to see the wood's surface getting shiny. You might also be able to hear the sound this makes.

Hissing

When you raise the handle, the edge starts to cut and as you move the tool along the wood a hissing sound is heard as well as the rubbing sound, if the bevel is still rubbing.

Raise the handle higher and the tool will want to remove a deeper shaving, which is great if you want to remove a lot of material. Keep the tool moving or it will dig-in.

Another way to remove a lot of waste is to cut very close to the point, as in the photo above.

When planing a long cylinder, you may find the tool cuts less efficiently

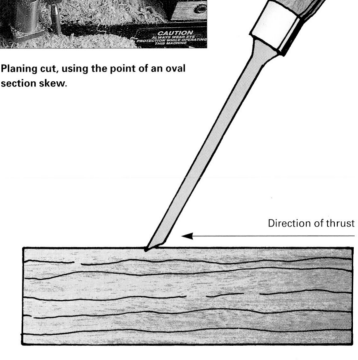

Direction of thrust

Attempted planing cut with a firmer chisel, the bevel not rubbing.

at the end of the cut than at the beginning. This is because you have not kept the same angle all the way along the toolrest.

As the angle changes, the edge loses contact with the work and if you are not removing timber when turning, it's a good idea to stop and work out why?

The best way to keep the angle the same is to hold the tool against the body and start with the weight on the right foot at the right-hand end of the cut. As the tool passes along the tool-rest, gradually transfer the weight to the left foot.

A very long cylinder will, of course, require more than one step, but I suggest you get the cut working smoothly on short lengths before adding the woodturner's sideways shuffle to your list of skills.

I get my pupils to do the planing cut with the right hand on the handle

when cutting to the left, and vice versa. It's useful to be able to use either hand in this way. If you try to be ambidextrous when you start turning, you will not get into the habit of thinking there is any difficulty in changing hands.

One direction

Most people find it easier to cut in one direction rather than another, but those right-handed are often surprised to find it easier to use the left hand on the handle.

There are no hard and fast rules about this, but it's a fact that both hands have work to do when turning. And you might as well transfer the tool from hand to hand rather than alter your stance.

Another common problem pupils have is making waves on the work's surface that cause the tool to vibrate yet resist the cutting power of the

Planing cut, with rectangular section skew.

Preventing flexing on a planing cut by using the hand.

Peeling cut.

edge. The surface may be smooth, but it isn't flat. In fact it is often shiny.

The first solution is the usual one of sharpening the chisel. This change of activity gives your muscles a chance to relax.

The main cause of ribbing is undue pressure on the bevel causing the edge to bounce away from the wood's surface. The answer is not to press harder, for this will cause the tool to follow the ribs, or waves.

You probably need to raise the bevel slightly from the surface and make the edge cut through the wave tops. Also, check that the toolrest is not too low, because if it is the edge is not well supported.

The waves are created by cutting with bad technique. They can often be removed by cutting correctly in the opposite direction. If this fails, a change of speed may help.

Ribbing affects even expert turners when a spindle is so thin it flexes away from the tool. One answer is to support the work by exterting an opposing force.

This can be done by means of a steady, a commercially available set of wheels, held in place on the opposite side of the work to the tool.

Alternatively, you can hold the work in the palm of one hand, with the thumb on the top of the tool to steady it, while most of the directing is done by the other.

Don't try this latter course of action until you have acquired sufficient

skills. It helps to prevent flexing away from the tool if you reduce the pressure between centres. One way of doing this is to hold the work in a four-jaw chuck instead of against a drive centre.

Peeling cut

This is exactly like the peeling cut done with the beading and parting tool, which I tend to use for this purpose rather than a skew. Its square end and flat faces make it easier to control and better at producing a square cut.

It is feasible to use a rectangular section skew for this cut, but not so easy with an oval section skew,

because the rounded faces are more difficult to keep steady.

The peeling cut is used to remove timber quickly, particularly to form spigots at the ends of spindles to avoid holes left by the centres remaining in the finished article. It also prevents the tool slipping onto the centres while turning.

The tool is presented to the wood with the edge parallel to the lathe's axis, so the tool shaft has to be angled. Cutting should be done at the point end of the edge. You should not try to cut with the whole of the edge at once, because this can be too heavy a cut and might stop the lathe.

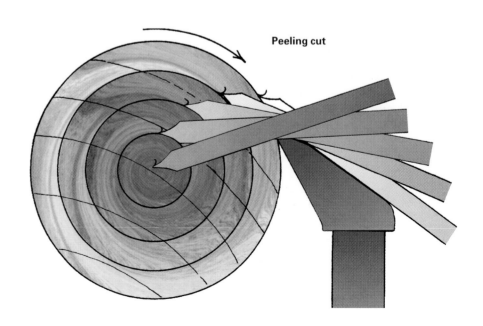

Peeling cut

Slicing cut.

Do not push the tool in horizontally, because it will ruin the edge and not cut efficiently. The tool should point upwards and the bevel should rest on the wood before the edge is brought into contact by raising the handle.

The tool will bite, but don't be faint-hearted. If you maintain pressure up and over the toolrest, the bevel will support the cut and you will peel off a clean shaving.

Slicing cuts

If you go back to the stationary piece of wood in the vice and try to clean up one end to make a perfect right-angle using a chisel, you will find you can do this only if the tool is very sharp.

Using a firmer chisel, you can clean up an already right-angled face either with the bevel or the flat face of the tool flush with the face. But if the tool surface is not flush, you produce ridges.

If you cut right across the face you will almost certainly break away a layer of fibres as the chisel finishes the cut, leaving a ragged edge. This is because the last few fibres are not supported – and why you should not cut against the grain.

This is not a problem when turning the end of a blank because it's difficult to get past the dead centre, but it's what happens when you try to cut uphill between centres.

When you use the slicing cut on the end of a blank held between centres, you need to avoid contact between the tool and the lathe centre. So it's best to turn a spigot first, using the peeling cut.

With the slicing cut, the bevel directs the cut's direction, as in the stationary example, but the actual cutting is done with a point.

If the skew has a straight edge, you can use either the toe or the heel, but if the edge is curved it's not so easy to use the heel, because it does not really come to a point.

The reason I use the toe is that it's easy to see what is happening, whereas when the heel is used it is hidden by the tool.

Before starting the lathe, hold the tool against the end of the blank with the toe on the tailstock centre and the bevel resting against the face. Provided the end is fairly square this gives the angle at which to hold the tool.

Right angles

If the end of the wood is at right angles to the lathe's axis the handle must point to one side. In this position, a large section of the edge will contact the face of the wood.

Avoid this when turning, because while the toe is cutting, the rest of the edge will also be trying to bury itself into the end. To stop this happening, move most of the edge slightly away from the face by rotating the tool. Just the tool does the cutting.

When you practise the slicing cut, you should present the point fairly high up and remove a sliver. When first trying this, there's a tendency to take too thick a cut. This usually results in the cut grinding to a halt part way down, as the point gets wedged into the wood.

If you cut too thickly, but still manage to complete it, you will leave a rough surface, so remember that it's a finishing cut and think microscopic.

Ribbed surface

Early attempts at this cut often leave a ribbed surface, which can look quite decorative, if that is what turns you on. But if you prefer a smooth effect that needs no sanding, you should make the point describe an arc on the outside of the face so that it goes up and then downwards towards the centre.

This makes the point cut all the way and does not allow the bevel to force the edge off the surface, which it will do if the angle of the handle is not maintained to keep the bevel at right angles to the axis.

These three cuts are the basis of shaping with the skew. In my next article I'll describe how to form beads and coves and give you some projects to practice. ■

Slicing cut.

Variations on a theme

O nce you've mastered the planing, peeling and slicing cuts with the skew chisel by repeated practice, the next step is to make some more elaborate shapes.

Most of the forms used in spindle turning are simply variations on a theme of beads and coves.

Cut a series of them on branches of about 50mm, 2in diameter by 150mm, 6in long. Continue until you can make them without too many catches.

Turning coves and beads with a skew chisel

Learning a skill

I'll go into detail about each catch later, but first I want to comment on acquiring a skill. I have just started to learn how to play the piano, having started with a teach yourself course, to see if I had any hope of being able to learn it.

When I felt I'd gone as far as I could with that, I decided I needed tuition. A friend who plays the piano but does not teach would have helped me, probably for nothing, but I decided against it. He would not know what exercises to recommend and would not be able to analyse where I was going wrong.

I went instead to a qualified teacher who charged £6 per half hour but who I felt would be worth it because I'd learn much quicker by being taught to do things properly.

Proper training

This proved to be true. I soon learnt how to sit correctly, how to hold my hands at the keyboard and how to stroke the keys.

I was given a book of exercises and told to practise slowly so that I played without mistakes, and gradually built up speed from a secure base.

My playing has increased by leaps and bounds since my weekly lessons began. I have also learned some useful teaching techniques.

I won't labour the analogy, because it's obvious that whatever skill you want to learn, the ways of practising are going to be similar.

Qualification

The big difference between learning to play the piano and turning is that there is a well-established teaching and examination system in music, so the criteria is there for evaluating prospective tutors.

But until we get a national vocational qualification in woodturning, tutors can only be chosen through personal recommendation, by their work, written pieces or demonstrations.

Look for evidence that the prospective tutor has analysed what he is doing and can not only communicate it clearly but explain why? Ensure his workshop is well-equipped and that you will have constant access to a lathe. Don't think a thorough grasp of technique somehow diminishes creativity. Just as you need to be able to play piano notes properly before you can make beautiful music, so you need tool skills to turn attractive items.

Beads

The most efficient way for me to turn a bead is with a skew chisel, because I've practised long and hard. I get a smooth shape which needs little sanding.

I get the occasional catch when my attention wanders, but the time lost in making good or starting again is made up in the speed achieved when things are going well.

If you are happy with another method, stick with it, because using the skew is not necessarily the easiest option.

Convert one of your 50mm, 2in branches to a cylinder using the spindle roughing gouge, and turn a spigot at both ends so you can avoid

The starting point for cutting a bead. The tip of the skew is cutting with the bevel rubbing behind. No other part of the tool touches the wood.

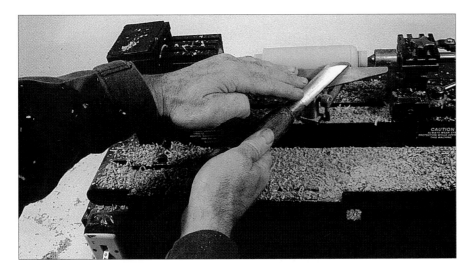

A longer shot of the start of a bead, showing the position of the tool handle. As the cut progresses, the handle is swept round. An oval skew developed by Robert Sorby is used to help the smooth rolling cut for beads.

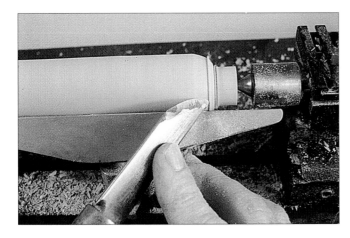

Part way round the bead, close up. Only the tip of the tool and the bevel just behind still touch the wood.

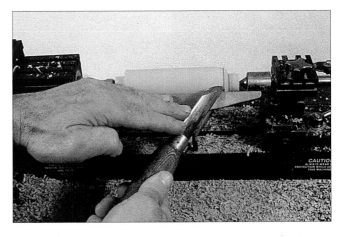

Part way round the tool overview. The tool has been rotated to follow the bead's curve and the handle starts its sweep round.

the centres with the tool. I cut beads with the point of the tool. Before you try it, rehearse the cut with the work at rest.

Each stage is pictured here in pairs – one close to the work to show the point of cut, and one from further back to show the position of the hands.

Follow these four procedures:

1. Hold the skew chisel with the wide face on the toolrest and the long point on the shoulder at the end of the cylinder with the edge of the tool parallel with the lathe's axis. You should be able to put part of the bevel flush against the work while the point also contacts the shoulder.
2. Move the handle towards your body while rotating the wrist clockwise, but keep the tool's point in contact with the work's shoulder.
3. Continue moving the tool in the same direction, gradually raising the handle.
4. At the end of the cut, rest the point on the junction between the spigot and the workpiece. The bevel should be flush against the end face of the work and the handle higher than the toolrest and pointing to the right about 65° to the axis.

To achieve a smooth shape this motion must be done in one sweep, without changing grip. This means the handle must be held at the start of

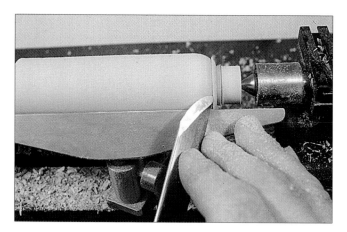

Towards the end of the bead, close up. The skew is rotated more onto its edge to follow the curve.

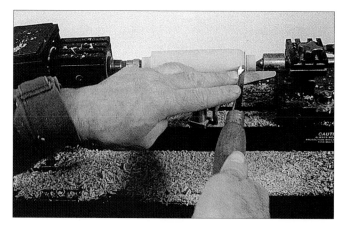

From further back, you can see that at this stage the handle is nearly at right angles to the lathe axis.

The end of the beading cut. The tip and the bevel still touch the wood, which is why the edge is just over on one side.

At the end of the cut, the handle has completed the sweep across the turner's body as the bevel follows the curve of the bead.

the cut, with the wrist rotated anti-clockwise as far as it will go.

When your action is smooth, start the lathe. Make the first cut about 6mm, ¼in from the shoulder. Don't start with the point in contact with the work but hold it as in photos, with the bevel rubbing.

Raise the handle slowly and as the point begins to cut, rotate the tool and continue to raise the handle until the tool ends with the bevel at right angles to the axis.

The knack

The trick is to manipulate the tool so that the point is cutting all the time and the edge behind the point does not snag the surface just made.

A common fault is to try to cut too deeply. This simply makes the tool wedge into the wood. This can also happen if the tool is rotated too quickly.

If the tool is not rotated fast enough the bevel rubs but the point is not in contact, so it doesn't cut. You know you are cutting all the way round a bead if there is a continuous furrow at the tip of the tool.

After the first couple of cuts, when the rounded shape begins to appear, you should aim for a surface that is a segment of a circle. This means the amount of wood you remove varies during the cut.

Start by cutting a sliver and gradually increase the amount as you near the middle of the cut, reducing its depth until it is thin again at the end. To round off the other end of the piece, you reverse the above.

To make a succession of beads, it's best to mark them with a pencil and cut the hollows in between with a beading and parting tool. Don't go too deep, or you will weaken the work.

If you make the distance between lines the diameter of the cylinder you are turning, the beads will look reasonably round when completed properly.

Coves

Start a cove by marking the middle with the point of the skew and create a vee by cutting first one side and then the other.

You will get accidental spirals unless the tool is lined up so that a bevel rubs on the side of the vee the tool is cutting.

This means that when you cut the right-hand side of the vee, the tool has to be tilted to the right with the handle over that side. It's reversed for the left-hand side.

The tool has to pass in front of your body when you change from side to side and this is one reason why spindle tools are not as long as bowl

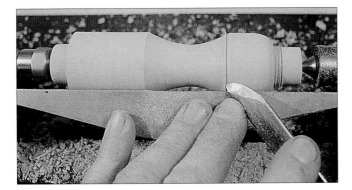
Starting the cove with the point of the skew.

Centre of right-hand side slope, cutting with edge.

Feathering off the cut in the middle of the cove.

Front view of cove cutting.

tools. When the vee cut is as deep as you want the cove to be (make your first efforts shallow), the profile has to be curved. Starting on the right, the tool enters the top of the vee with the point taking a thin cut.

Hold the tool slightly more vertical than when doing the side of the vee, because you need to increase the depth of cut as you progress down the slope until you reach half-way. Then you begin to decrease the depth of cut by laying the tool slightly on its side, so the bevel is closer to the surface.

After the first entry of the point, the cutting is taken over by the edge just behind it. The tool must stop cutting as it reaches the cove's centre, because it would be bad news to try cutting uphill. The photo of me sensibly wearing a respirator helmet was taken from the other side of the lathe to show the position of both hands.

It's a good exercise to round off both ends of a blank and then make a series of coves, aiming for uniformity of shape. When you have mastered the shallow cove, you can practice making them narrower in gradual stages.

Rolling pins

Rolling pins can be made in a wide variety of sizes and styles. They were traditionally made of beech or sycamore, though my mother's soft-wood version lasted many years.

To get the handles the same at both ends, be it just a round bead or a longer handle shape, the trick is to work at both ends alternately, so each adjustment to the shape is a small one. Radical changes of design are only required in response to major disasters. ■

A simple rolling pin. The handles are just two beads side-by-side. Each shoulder is one side of a v-cut.

Cutting coves

How to cut deep narrow coves with a skew chisel

I started to turn full time at a craft centre in Devon where I quickly realised that I had to make small cheap items. The clientele were tourists and I needed to earn money with little outlay. So, I had to quickly convert small bits of wood into things people would buy.

This meant turning between centres and, having seen an expert in action, I knew a skew chisel was the best tool for the job. But, it was not easy to master the skew.

I called upon all my resources of bloody-minded determination and kept trying. I'd get it right sometimes then get a catch without knowing why. Trying to recover the knack would get me so frustrated, I'd abandon the lathe for a time.

Expensive tutor

The lessons were learnt, courtesy of an expensive tutor – time. I eventually got to the stage where, after I'd roughed out with a spindle roughing gouge, I would only use the skew.

Indeed, I did not own a proper spindle gouge for years and only taught myself to use it correctly when I had to teach this to others.

Whatever shape I needed, I did it with a skew, gradually developing a

Cove showing rough finish on the left side, where the cutting edge is supported by the bevel rubbing on the uneven shoulder of the cove.

way of cutting deep narrow coves with one. I've not heard of anyone else doing this, but if you have I'd be pleased to hear of it.

This technique enables you to make narrower coves than with a spindle gouge. But, it is only possible after lots of practice with the skew. When turning deep and narrow coves with the point down, at the bottom of the cove the cutting edge is not supported by the bevel next to the edge. It is supported by the shoulder of the bevel resting on the shoulder of the cove.

Prove this to yourself by roughing out a blank of cheap waste wood so that the right-hand end is cylindrical and the left-hand end still has flats. Cut a cove between the sections with a skew chisel, point down, using the method described last month (*Woodturning* 54).

As the cove gets deeper, the side next to the smooth cylinder (right) should get a good finish from the

Entering a narrow cove, skew chisel point down, bevel at right-angles to the axis.

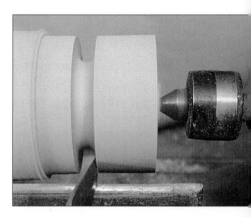

As the cut progresses, tilt the skew to the left to avoid the edge catching on the shoulder.

As the point goes deeper into the cove the tool goes up and over the toolrest.

tool, but the other side (left) should not. The roughness of the cove shoulder will be reflected in the surface achieved by the tool. If this does not happen, then the cove is not deep or narrow enough.

To get close-up photographs of this use of the skew, I converted an old 38mm, 1½in scraper into a skew (I don't normally use one bigger than 25mm, 1in) and mounted a piece of sycamore 75 x 75 x 300mm, 3 x 3 x 12in between centres. It has taken me a while to realise it's cheaper to double the size of little projects rather than buy a new lens for the camera.

After roughing out the blank start the cove with a narrow v-groove, cut with the point of the skew. Deepen this by slicing cuts, alternately on each side, until you nearly reach the required depth.

Narrow cove

To get the straight sides and rounded bottom, enter the point of the tool at the top of the v-cut with the bevel lined up at right angles to the axis of the lathe. The photos have been taken with the camera higher than eye level, so you can see what happens at the bottom of the cove.

Instead of following the sloping sides of the vee, use the point to cut straight down. The trick is to avoid the edge catching on the side you have just cut. Do this by concentrating on tilting the tool to the left, so there is always daylight between the edge

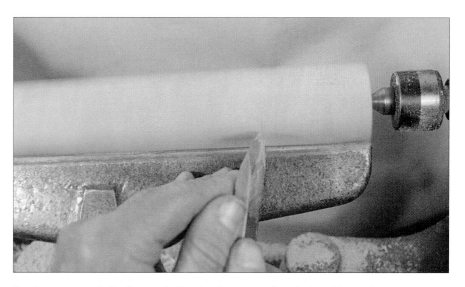

Cutting a pommel, the first cut is like that for a v-cut, but the bevel is nearly at right-angles to the axis.

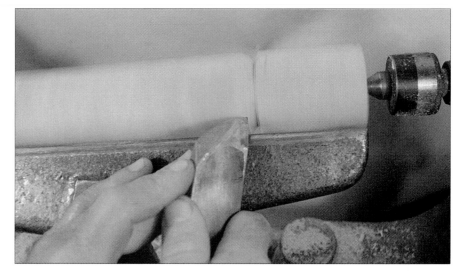

The second cut for a pommel – the other side of a v-cut.

To cut the cove, edge support comes from the shoulder of the bevel and the shoulder of cove.

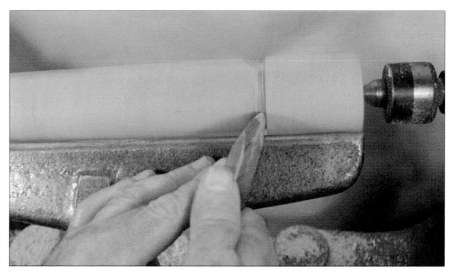

The cut widens as it get deeper, each right-angle cut getting closer to the marked pommel.

A finished straight faced pommel with cylinder roughed to round.

and the side of the cove while the point is cutting.

Take care with this cut, as a catch will ruin the shoulder of the cove and may cause the wood to escape from the lathe. Face protection from a face-mask, Racal Airstream helmet or similar is advisable when turning, but especially so when trying this cut for the first time.

As the tool gets further down the side of the cove, the end of the handle is raised so the point can carry on cutting. At the bottom you want to convert from vee to rounded. The point cannot cut sideways as required, so slide the point past the cutting zone (by now it is well below the level of the tool rest) and cut with the edge. This should be moved from right to left shaping as it goes.

To achieve a smooth finish you, naturally, cut downhill. So the left-hand side has to be cut from the left down to the centre of the cove.

Shoulder support

You would expect the edge to be cutting without support at this stage, but if the bevel's shoulder is rubbing on the shoulder of the cove it will give all the support needed. Again, it's essential to avoid the edge coming into contact with the shoulder of the cove.

The only occasion when this method of turning a narrow cove cannot be used is when you need to turn one next to a pommel (a part of a spindle that is square in section). Unfortunately, it's where designers with a grudge against turners often want them.

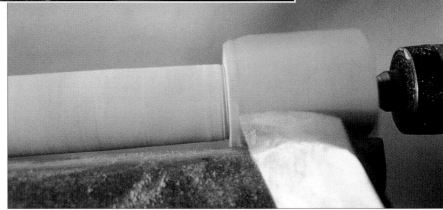

Starting to round the pommel corner is similar to rounding a cylinder, but the bevel cannot rub all the way round.

As rounding the pommel progresses, the tip cuts back to solid wood all the way round.

As turning spindles with pommels isn't easy, I'll explain how I do them.

It's vital to plane the blank before you start. Something obvious to me now, but not before my first run of balusters. Much time can be wasted trying to plane them after turning and you will never get it right.

You need to mount the blank accurately, since you cannot true up the square section once you have started turning. Many spindles have pommels at both ends with turned features between. I mark the pommels with a pencil and set-square on two faces of the blank, then cut them before roughing out the cylindrical section and marking out the turned features.

The problem with pommels is that if you make a mistake the blank is ruined, so rule number one is to make some spare blanks. If you are working for a furniture maker who has already cut joints in the spindles you rarely

BELOW: **Cutting a cove next to a pommel has to be done with a spindle gouge.**

get spares – the pressure can get unbearable.

Rule number two is keep the tool-rest clear of the square edges and never adjust it without stopping the lathe. Rule three is never start the cut on the line, for as you insert the tool it will act as a wedge and break out the corners.

Experience on turning cylinders is needed to cut pommels. You have to line up the tool as though the blurred outer edge of the square blank is a solid cylinder.

The first cut for a pommel is about 25mm, 1in from the line. The bevel is nearly at right angles to the lathe axis because the aim is to produce a v-cut with the right side of the vee almost at the same angle as the face of the pommel.

The next cut is with the skew tilted over to open out the v-cut. You progress opening and deepening the vee until you reach the solid wood, ie the diameter of the maximum cylinder available.

Cut pommel face

When you have achieved this, you can cut the pommel face. Remove thin cuts, at right angles to the axis and perfectly flat. The cutting is all done with the point of the skew, so the edge of the skew has to be slightly tilted to stop it catching the face of the pommel.

It's difficult to achieve a flat face with straight edges. If this doesn't happen my first move is to sharpen the tool. If this does not work the fault may lie with the type of skew. The skew has to be rectangular in section so the flat side gives maximum

support on the tool rest.

If the fault persists, then it is down to technique and you must check the bevel is as near to right angles with the axis as is possible and that the point is going up and then over the toolrest and down as the cut progresses.

The straight-faced pommel is not very user friendly. The corners are commonly rounded, using the point of the skew as though the square edges of the pommel were a solid cylinder, but not quite resting the bevel on them. The support provided would be more rhythmic than useful.

If you are used to forming normal beads the cut is not a problem, provided you are brave.

For a narrow cove next to the pommel you can do the initial v-cut with a skew. Because the square edges of the pommel provide such poor support you have to round the bottom of the cove with a narrow spindle gouge. Start this cut with the gouge on its side and as it progresses rotate the tool so it finishes at the bottom of the cove with the flute pointing up.

Once you have turned the pommels, the cylindrical section in between can

be roughed out with a spindle roughing gouge and the details added using a skew.

The main problem with this sort of turning is the flexing that occurs because of the thinness of the spindle and the pressure from the centres.

This manifests itself in chattering, making a series of spirals. Flexing can be solved using a proprietary steady which supports the spindle in the middle, or you can use your hand wrapped around the spindle as it rotates.

Limitations

The latter method should only be tried by advanced turners and has limitations when pommels are present. Pommels should not be touched under any circumstances when the piece is rotating.

Wherever possible, I like to hold spindles in an Axminster four-jaw chuck (external jaws). I don't have to apply so much pressure from the tail-centre and flexing is much reduced.

Next month, I'll talk about turning rings with the skew and some of my own modifications of this versatile tool. ∎

The original rattle as it appeared in the Design Council index.

Ring rattle

Using the skew chisel to make a captive rings rattle

Twenty years ago, while casting around for ideas of small saleable articles to make, a colleague suggested a child's rattle. Traditionally, this consisted of a box with peas in it, on a stick. But box-making was too big a struggle for me to consider making them on a production basis. So I rejected the idea.

Then one night I had a flash of inspiration – how about a rattle of captive rings on a stick? I experimented at the lathe and made one. It proved popular with the public and was selected for the Design Council's index.

Chuffed

I was chuffed to be able to attach the council's distinctive black and white label to the rattle and to see it pictured in the index. My original design has since changed from five 'washers' on a stick, to three 'doughnuts', but the basic idea is still the same.

It looks similar to rattles other turners have made, being an obvious response to a given design brief by a simple method of production, ie. turning.

I stopped making them on a production basis when new regulations made the testing of children's toys offered for sale obligatory and expensive. The principle of making a loose ring with a skew chisel is simply

The handle, stopper and the first ring of this rattle have been cut. One corner of the second ring has been cut as a bead and continues round to start undercutting.

Making space for the tool by reducing the waste on the shaft.

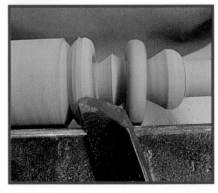

A v-cut has been made and the second side of the ring is being cut.

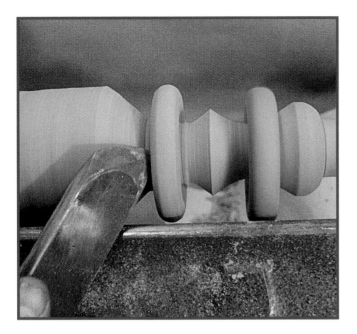
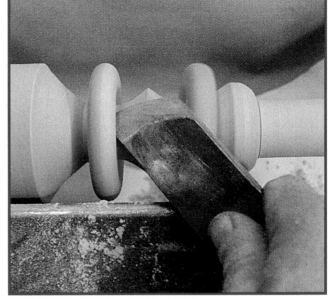

The rounding-over cut continues under the ring, undercutting it.　　　**Undercutting continues until...**

that of making a bead and undercutting it. It sounds simple, and most of my spindle pupils cut loose rings within a day of being taught the skew. But it's another matter to produce them quickly, with a consistent profile and close together on a rattle.

Safety

A blank measuring 38 x 38 x 140mm (1 ½ x 1 ½ x 5 ½in) produces a rattle small enough for a baby to hold but not so small it can choke on it.

I often use European ash *(Fraxinus excelsior)*, but sycamore *(Acer pseudoplatanus)* is also good. I tend to avoid poisonous timbers like yew *(Taxus baccata)* and tambootie *(Spirostachys africana)*.

The skew chisel I use is a Sorby 19mm (¾in) oval section with a curved edge, as this has a thin section for getting under the overhang. But any other make of oval skew will do as well.

I rough the blank to a cylinder with a spindle roughing gouge and reduce the handle section to about half the original. It will·be about one-third the length of the rattle.

I turn a spigot at the end of the handle, near the live centre, to enable me to turn away the hole left by it's point. Then I round the end of the handle, as though it were a bead,

using the point of the skew.

I make a v-cut at the place where the stopper meets the handle, so I can reduce the diameter of the part that will be the stopper with a peeling cut. I then round the right-hand end of the stopper to a curve like that of the handle's end.

The handle is formed using the skew long point down, cutting just behind the point. The finished diameter should be about a third of the original.

Flowing

The curve of the skew enables the handle's concave shape to be turned in one flowing movement. Control is needed when you meet the stopper, because contact with the point will bring rapid design changes.

The first ring is formed as near the stopper as possible, allowing for room to get the skew chisel under the ring. The right-hand face of the potential ring left by the peeling cut will be fairly ragged, but a few slicing cuts with the point of the skew should clean this up and produce the necessary gap.

The slicing cuts can go below the maximum diameter of the stopper, because the right-hand side of the ring will have to be undercut below the top of the stopper or the captive

ring will no longer be captive. The left-hand side of the ring starts with a v-cut made by the skew down to the diameter of the handle. The square top of the ring can be converted to a bead by rounding each side.

The undercut is done by continuing the rounding cut under the bead with the uppermost bevel rubbing on the underface providing the support for the tool.

It is the point of the skew which does all the cutting. When the tool won't go any further because it is wedged into the gap, you enlarge the aperture. It's like opening one side of a v-cut.

I work on one side of the ring and then the other, until I judge that it's about to break through. It's important not to force the tool into the gap, because you can cause the ring to break away, leaving a rough underside and burning the surface of the ring.

Separate

Before separating the ring, it's best to sand it. If the join between ring and body is narrow, you can separate the two with a clean cut from the skew chisel and there should be no need to sand that part.

Babies tend not to be critical of these things. Their first use of the rattle

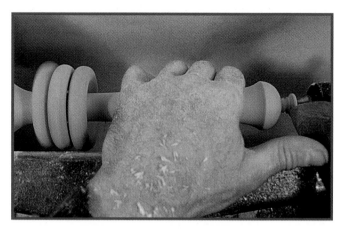

ABOVE: **Reduce the waste at the tailstock end to the minimum to save finishing time off the lathe.**

BELOW: **Part off the headstock end with the skew chisel. Hold the work lightly to avoid burning.**

...breakthrough, the ring is parted.

is usually to put it in their mouth, the second to throw it to the floor.

When all rings have been freed, the shaft can be smoothed with the skew. You might think the rings would get in the way, but they move away from the tool, provided they are not caught with the edge. I hold them out of the way with one hand and hold the skew in the other - but that takes practice.

Wholeness

When the shaft is smooth, the end needs to be rounded. To achieve a wholeness of design, it should be the same shape as the other end.

I usually put no finish on a rattle because of its destination, but if you want to improve the appearance an edible finish such as walnut oil from the supermarket is advisable.

I part the completed rattle with the skew point, cutting cleanly and as far as possible. It means less finishing has to be done off the lathe. To do this you have to support the rattle with one hand and hold the tool in the other. Don't grip too tightly, for the smell of burning flesh can be offensive.

The end furthest from the lathe is reduced to a fine point first. Because the rotational force is being transmitted through the headstock end, leave this thick as long as possible.

Judging when the junction will break involves learning the strength of the wood. This comes with experience. Every so often I'm caught out by a sample which is softer than expected, but that's usually when I'm not concentrating, because by parting off time you should know the strength of the wood.

For rings on smaller items such as lace bobbins and Trunnion boxes, I've developed a hooked tool (see drawing on p.66) which can do the business in the most confined spaces.

On my visits to turning clubs I've been shown several answers to the same problem. They all work, I'm sure, because all you need is a point at the end of a curved shaft, thin enough to get under the ring yet strong enough not to bend.

Sorby's latest ring tools work well and, in use with their bead forming tool, enable rings of a consistent size and round cross-section to be made. But you have to buy a different set for each size of ring you want to make, so it's not as flexible as using a skew. Don't try to make a hooked shaped tool from a thin parting tool, as I did, because there is not enough strength in the shaft to support the force put upon the cutting point.

Here endeth the lesson about the skew. But it will return! ■

The completed rattle.

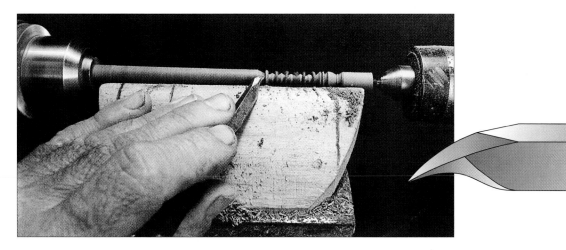

Parting off a small ring using my hooked ring tool.

Hooked ring tool.

Single-bevel skews

It's not difficult to make the separating cut with a normal skew, provided the distance between the rings is big enough. But I keep the rings as close as possible to keep the rattle small, and have developed a tool for this.

As the problem is the narowness of the gap, I made single-bevel skews which are about half as thin as skews with two bevels. I made them from second-hand carving chisels bought from junk shops, or outlets such as Tools UK. I believe they are now being marked by Crown Tools for cabinetmakers.

The tools are used just for the final parting of the ring and are specific to one side only. The cutting is done with the long point, and the bevel supports the cut by rubbing on the rattle's shaft.

I also use these tools for parting off where there is not enough room to introduce a two-bevel skew. But you must be cautious when using them, as there is less room for error than with a traditional skew.

These single-bevel skews, ground from carving tools, are used to undercut rings which are closely spaced.

A single-bevel skew in action. The bevel rubs on the shaft of the work.

An axe to grind

It's not the tool that does the turning.

Photo 1 **Roughing cut with felling axe.**

When I first saw Del Stubbs demonstrate with an axe, 10 years ago, he was seeking to show that it's not the tool that does the turning, but a sharp edge and skill. It was a spectacular way to start a demonstration, a dynamic way to make a point.

I often use an axe in my own demonstrations, having practised in my workshop with the full head protection only an Airstream helmet gives.

The secret

The secret, as with all cutting tools, is that as long as the edge is sharp and the bevel concave, you use it as though it were a large skew chisel with an inconvenient handle. I make sure the edge is curved and the point sharp by grinding on the wide, unencumbered wheel of a Tormek.

The roughing can be done with a tree felling axe (photo 1), using the edge near the point and the point facing downwards. The handle will catch on the floor if you try it with the point up.

A beast

I have used this beast to turn a ring, but the weight is such that the cut tends to carry on after you intended to stop, so I use a hatchet for detailed work.

Photo 2 shows a smoothing cut being made with this smaller axe. Note how the ends are more safely

turned by cutting from the centre outwards, as it's difficult to begin the cut right at the end.

This cut can be tried with the point up, but I find the way shown to be easier, since the end of the handle can be seen at all times and is therefore unlikely to unexpectedly hit me where it hurts.

For rapid removal of material (such as when forming a spigot at the end of

Photo 2 **Smoothing cut with hatchet.**

the piece) it's effective to use a peeling cut with the edge fairly parallel to the lathe's axis (see photo 3 over page).

As with the beading and parting tool, the bevel can be rested on the surface of the work before the handle is slowly raised and the edge contacts. At this point the edge is pushed up and over the toolrest in an arc which, if carried to its conclusion, would end at the centre of the wood. ➤

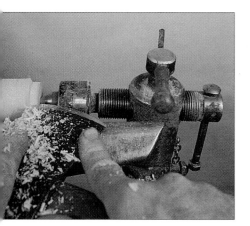

Photo 3 **Peeling cut.**

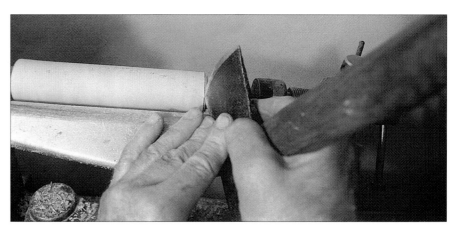

Photo 4 **Slicing cut.**

The slicing cut is used to give a mirror finish to the end grain (see photo 4). The cutting is done with the point and the bevel must line up with the direction of cut.

Since the end is at right angles to the axis, the body of the axe must be presented at the angle to achieve this. The axe handle will then be pointing over the right shoulder.

You start the cut with the point fairly high on the work, and push the tool up over the rest and then down towards the centre. Take care to ensure the edge does not catch the end grain as the cut progresses.

The slicing cut is used to form beads and their ultimate extension rings (see photo 5). The cutting is done with the point, and the tool is started almost flat on the rest but ends in the same position as in photo 4.

Always tackle the corner of the proto-bead first and do a series of cuts towards the peak of the bead. Remove a little at a time, to leave a smooth surface and don't wedge the tool in a deep groove.

After forming the left-hand side of the ring (photo 6), undercut the ring with the top bevel rubbing against the underside (photo 7). Take a little off each side until the ring breaks loose.

If the axe won't go any further into the underhang, remove more wood from the stem which will support the ring. If you try to force the axe under the ring it will burn the wood or even break the ring.

Using an axe in this way will soon teach you why turning tools are

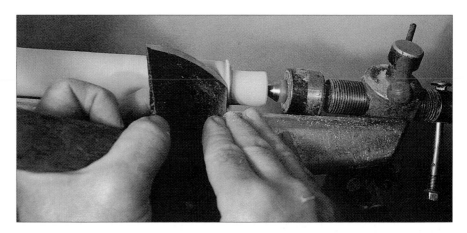

Photo 5 **Forming a ring.**

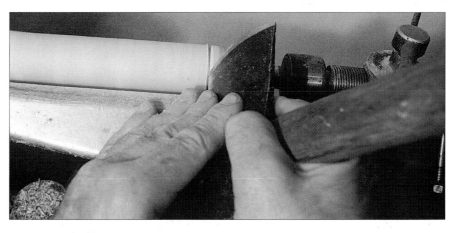

Photo 6 **Left-hand side of ring.**

developed as they are – the axe head is hard to hold and the junction between thumb and palm soon gets sore.

Parting tools

In a previous article on parting, I kept the number of tools in my recommended tool starter kit to a minimum by not including a dedicated parting tool, for parting can be done with a beading and parting tool, which has other uses as well.

I usually part off with a skew chisel, because I can shape the ends of the pieces while parting them and leave a very clean finish. At times, however, you may want to part off with less wastage than you get with the beading

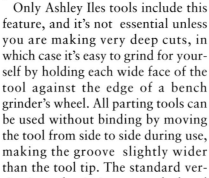

Photo 7 **Undercutting the ring.**

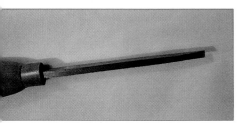

Photo 8 **Standard parting tool, from Robert Sorby, circa 1975.**

Photo 9 **Fluted parting tool.**

Photo 10 **Crown Tools' thin parting tool.**

Parting Tools

Standard Parting Tool

Diamond Parting Tool

Fluted Parting Tool

Thin Parting Tool

The tool in the photo is an old one and is relieved behind the edge so that the sides don't bind after the edge has passed into the wood.

Only Ashley Iles tools include this feature, and it's not essential unless you are making very deep cuts, in which case it's easy to grind for yourself by holding each wide face of the tool against the edge of a bench grinder's wheel. All parting tools can be used without binding by moving the tool from side to side during use, making the groove slightly wider than the tool tip. The standard version is used pointing up, so the bevel supports the cut, and as you progress you push the tool up and over the toolrest (see photo 11). Don't get into the habit of pushing the tool

and parting tool or skew chisel. Dedicated parting tools are the answer, of which there are four main types: standard (photo 8), diamond, fluted (photo 9) and thin (photo 10).

The standard type is made from rectangular stock with two long bevels at the end. It comes in two widths – 6 and 9mm (¼ and ⅜in).

Photo 11 **The standard parting tool in use.**

Photo 12 **Groove produced by the standard parting tool.**

Photo 13 **The fluted parting tool in action, with flute downwards.**

Photo 14 **The thin parting tool is used with the short bevel down**.

horizontally into the work, as it does not cut efficiently this way and soon blunts the edge.

A disadvantage of the standard tool can be seen in photo 12, where the ragged edge of the cut is evident. The faces of the groove are equally rough, showing why this tool has not worn down after 20 years in my collection.

Diamond

The diamond section parting tool is another answer to the problem of binding sides. It's so constructed that the widest part is at the cutting edge, tapering down on both sides.

The diamond is better for grooves than the standard type, but gives no cleaner edges.

Fluted

The fluted version is the one which gives clean sides to a parting cut. The tool has a semi-circular flute down the long side and a 45° bevel. It's used with the flute downwards (see photo 13), but like all peeling cuts works best with an up and over action.

You do not need to sharpen the flute, but you do the bevel, to keep the points sharp.

The entire bevel should be ground to retain the 45° angle. So long as the tool is sharp, the edges of the cut are

clean. The bottom of the groove produced always has a bead, which is no problem in a parting cut.

If you want a bead of that size as a decorative surface feature, this is a quick and easy way to produce it.

As the flutes' sharp corners can mark the toolrest, I only use this tool where I need a groove of this size with clean edges, or want a bead. It's no big hassle to file the toolrest now and then if it does get grooved.

Thin

The thin parting tool was originally made from hacksaw blades, by Chris Stott I believe. It's now marketed by tool makers because it's so effective.

The profile supplied is best modfied by grinding an extra-short bevel and making the long bevel concave, as in photo 10.

It's used with the short bevel down (see photo 14) and produces a very narrow groove with smooth sides.

It is useful for all parting, especially box lids, where its narrow cut creates least interruption of the grain pattern between lid and body and little need for a cleaning cut after parting.

Photo 15 shows the ring made by the axe and the two grooves produced by the fluted and thin parting tools. ■

Photo 15 **Ring produced by axe, and grooves made by thin and fluted parting tools.**

On end

End grain hollowing

You need to answer the following questions before you start turning a piece. What do I want to make? What is it going to look like? What is the sequence of operations? What timber will I use? Which way is the grain going to run? It's only when you have answered the last question that you can select your tools.

If the grain is running parallel to the lathe's axis you will need spindle tools (spindle roughing gouge, spindle gouge, skew, parting tool and perhaps a scraper). If the grain is running at right angles to the lathe, you'll need a bowl gouge and perhaps a scraper.

This is because the way you cut wood depends on the direction of the grain and turning tools are designed for specific jobs.

Bowl gouges are long and strong with long handles, because they are used to reach deep into large bowls where the grain is running at right angles to the lathe bed.

Spindle tools are shorter and not so heavily built because they don't usually have to project so far over the toolrest. Their handles are short, as the leverage a long handle gives is not needed, so they can pass in front of

the body. When I started turning, I thought my 50mm (2in) spindle roughing gouge ought to remove timber quicker from a bowl than a 13mm (½in) bowl gouge. I tried it and found it didn't work. You only cut with one small part of the edge, so all that extra length of edge is redundant.

It's also dangerous to use the spindle roughing gouge on bowls, because the points at the end of the edge can catch the surface of the wood, with potentially disastrous results.

Dicey

It's equally dicey to use a skew chisel on the outside of a normal bowl. It is hard enough controlling the tool on either side grain or end grain when turning a spindle, but in the case of a bowl where you are cutting both sorts of grain twice per revolution it's near impossible, and catches.

Catches with this tool on a large piece of timber would result in either a ruined piece or in a flying missile with an unpredictable landing point.

So if you have decided to make a goblet, a box, a scoop, or a small

end grain bowl where the grain runs parallel to the lathe's axis, don't hollow the end with a bowl gouge, cutting from outside to in, because it doesn't work.

You are cutting against the grain and even if you chip out the wood, it's hard work and the finish given by the tool will be rough.

To cut with the grain, you need to drill a central hole to the depth you wish to excavate and then cut from the inside out. The best tool for this job is the spindle gouge with a ground-back edge (see issue 51).

Items made from end grain relate to the nature of the wood. In the case of a goblet or scoop you need the longitudinal strength of the grain in

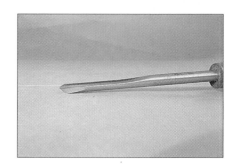

Spindle gouge with longer bevel on left hand side.

Blank for making a scoop, in the O'Donnell jaws of an Axminster four-jaw chuck.

the handle or stem. Boxes with this grain direction are made because shrinkage or expansion across the end grain is less than elsewhere, and this keeps the lid fitting well in spite of humidity changes.

If you make a box by hollowing into side grain it will tend to go oval if its moisture content changes, and the lid will tend to bend, exposing the joint between it and the body.

Small bowls of, say, 100 x 100 x 50mm (4 x 4 x 2in) are made from end grain because it is more efficient to mount a 100mm square x 175mm (7in) blank in a chuck and turn three bowls 'in the stack' than to mount three blanks one after the other.

Chucking

How you hold the work on the lathe is also influenced by the grain direction. To use ordinary screws into end grain is not safe, and long screws would waste wood and be inefficient for small items.

Single screw chucks are not suitable for the same reason, while expanding chucks will tend to split the wood. So compression chucks are the best option.

Most turners have a proprietary chuck which has a compression option. Turn a spigot to fit the jaws.

If you are not in this fortunate position, it's cheap to make a cup chuck by mounting a blank of dense timber such as hornbeam (which is not prone to splitting) on a faceplate and turning a tapered hole through it. Turn a matching taper on the blank and drive the blank into the hole with a hammer.

Sugar or salt bowl

If you haven't hollowed end grain before, I suggest you make a shallow bowl. Don't use a long blank, so

Shaping the bowl end of the scoop.

avoiding having a long projection from the chuck, which can prove unstable if you have a catch.

A 75 x 75 x 75mm (3 x 3 x 3in) blank would be ideal, in any hardwood of your choice, ash, sycamore or a fruitwood being especially suitable.

Set the lathe speed to about 1,450 rpm and, having mounted the blank between centres, rough out with the spindle roughing gouge. Use a beading and parting tool and callipers or a spanner to turn the correct size spigot.

If you often use use the chuck in compression mode, it makes sense to keep a secondhand spanner of the correct size in your chuck box.

When the blank is on the chuck, you will probably need to true it. Use the spindle roughing gouge on the side of the blank and the skew on the end.

Establish the bowl's depth by cutting a groove with a parting tool, so that there's a stem of about 38mm (1½in) diameter, and shape the outside with a skew or spindle gouge.

Place the toolrest across the end of the blank, as close to it as possible and at a height that will enable the gouge's nose to touch the centre of the blank when the tool is held horizontally.

Start the lathe and ease the gouge into the wood frequently withdraw-

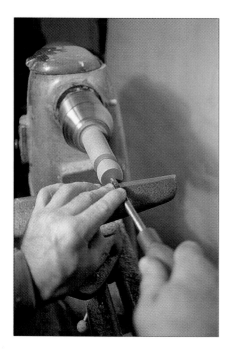

Starting hollowing with a gouge.

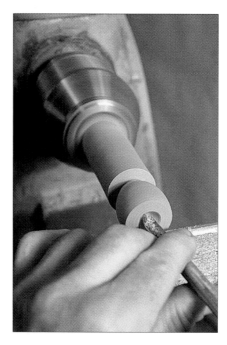

Moving the gouge tip to the left.

ing it to remove wood from the flute. If you have problems drilling a hole in this way, a drill bit in a Jacob's chuck in the tailstock will work, provided you are working on the inboard side.

When the hole is as deep as you want, less a margin for error, use the gouge to hollow it out, as in the project below.

Scoop

The wooden scoop is a signature piece of Richard Raffan, who showed me how to make them in 1975, when I didn't have the skills needed.

When I did, I'd forgotten how he did them, so I developed my own method, but chucked them in Richard's way by roughing out the blanks in big batches to fit the hollow spindle of my Graduate lathe and then driving them in with a hammer.

I now use the 50mm (2in) spigot diameter O'Donnell jaws of the Axminster four-jaw chuck, which need no roughing out. The ash blank used in the photos is 41 x 41 x 150mm (1 ⅝ x 1 ⅝ x 150in).

Having roughed out the blank and turned the end, turn the scoop's outer shape with a skew. Don't turn the stem to its final diameter, because this would not give enough support when hollowing the end. Note how the end

is slightly rounded so that the scoop scoops. Position the toolrest at the end and you can drill a hole to establish the depth, although in this instance I didn't.

At the start of hollowing, the tool should be held horizontally and rotated slightly so that the left-hand side of the gouge is a bit lower than the right.

The tip of the tool enters the work and the hollowing is effected by the left-hand side cutting as the tool is pivoted about a point on the toolrest.

Reducing wall thickness.

In other words, the tool tip moves to the left as the right hand moves to the right and is pulled outwards.

Grip the handle near the ferrule and rest the handle against your arm for extra support. As hollowing progresses, check you don't go too deep by using a pencil as a depth gauge.

I go to the full depth early on and then shape the inside to get an even wall thickness. I check this with the finger and thumb callipers (one of the cheaper makes, but not easily replace if badly damaged).

The thickness can also be checked by holding a lamp close to the work – if you can read the bulb wattage through the walls, they're too thin.

Evenness

It's important to achieve evenness, because one side will be cut away later, revealing every ridge and furrow. As the wall gets thinner, hold your fingers against the outside to absorb vibration, or you will get chattering inside.

Hold the tool on the toolrest with the thumb. The support of the arm on the handle will give it stability.

Because the bevel does not support the cut, it does not leave a very smooth finish. So I usually follow with a few passes of the half-round scraper, again supported with the

Smoothing with a scraper.

fingers on the outside of the bowl. This scraper has a 50° bevel sharpened on the Tormek grinder. I then clean up the top face on the side of the wheel which I have smoothed with the stone grader, removing any burr, and then clean the bottom face, so the tool moves freely over the rest.

I've long felt that the burr thrown up by a benchgrinder does not help a scraper's cutting action and that a sharp edge gives a cleaner finish. This has now been proved by Robbie Farrance's microscopic studies.

Shape the stem

When the inside has been hollowed, shape the stem using the skew. There's a flange where the bowl meets the stem, a decorative feature to punctuate the change of direction at this point. It's common on goblets and spindles and can be a bead of whatever shape you like.

Remove most of the bulk with the point of the skew. If the chuck is near the end of the scoop, use the skew heel down to get the required shape.

Sand your scoop and apply cooking oil to bring up the wood's colour without harming the user.

I part off with the point of the skew, supporting the scoop with the left hand. Because the end tapers to a point, no further sanding should be needed off the lathe.

You can shape the outside of the scoop with a linisher, sanding disc or saw. I don't recommend using a band

Using a pencil to check depth.

Shaping the stem with the point of the skew.

The finishing cut on the stem, with the skew heel down.

saw with a three-tooth skip blade, as it will shatter the end of a fine-walled scoop.

Hundreds of scoops will have to be made to get up to speed. It's only when you get up to six an hour that it becomes profitable. That's how much work a professional turner has to put in to become efficient.

If you can only make one an hour, but still sell them at a competetive price, you are working at a loss. To be able to eat, drink and pay the rent while doing that, requires another source of income. ■

Better bowls *Part One*

The bowl gouge

A salad bowl in olive ash, by Dave Regester, 350 x 100mm (14 x 4in).

When I started this series, I suggested a basic tool kit that included a 9mm (⅜in) bowl gouge, having found it big enough for most beginners' bowl-turning aspirations. Bowls as big as 355 x 350 x 100mm (14 x 13¾ x 4in) can be turned with ease using one of these.

My workhorse bowl gouge is the 13mm (½in) for smaller bowls and the 19mm (¾in) for those over 250mm (9¾in) wide, but the cost-conscious may prefer the 9mm (⅜in) bowl gouge, which is significantly cheaper.

The make of tool comes down to personal preference and price, because shapes vary. In the photos I'm using a 9mm (⅜in) Crown Tools' gouge, which is fine in this size, but I prefer Sorby tools for larger sizes, because their flutes are deeper and wider.

Bowl gouges are supplied with a

The 9mm (⅜in) bowl gouge from Crown Tools.

straight-across grind, which is easy to sharpen because it is just rolled on the bench grinder toolrest. Later, I'll devote an article to the mysteries of bowl gouge sharpening and a review of the jigs available, but for now just remember the basic rules of maintaining a hollow-ground bevel and a smooth edge.

If you want more information on this quickly, study Part Two of this series, my first book *Woodturning: Step by Step*, or my article on the

subject in *Woodturning Techniques* in *The Very Best From Woodturning* series.

As long as you apply the two rules mentioned, you should be able to produce shavings, but the angle of bevel and the profile of the edge can be altered to make things easier.

In other words, you can turn a bowl adequately with a straight-across grind but there are advantages in changing the profile. You can best appreciate these if you have first used the straight-across grind, so I'll introduce the ground-back profile later.

The wood used in the photos is unseasoned ash with a moisture content of 28%. I selected it because it had unsightly grey streaks which made it unsaleable as a finished bowl. It is 150mm (6in wide) and at the start was 100mm (4in deep).

I strongly recommend that you use such a piece to practise technique before thinking of finishing a bowl, so that you can try to get the angles at which you hold the tool correct without worrying about wasting wood.

If it turns out a reasonable shape when you have finished playing around and has a wall thickness of about 15mm (⅝ins), you can leave it to dry somewhere cool and re-turn it in a month or four when it should be dry.

I don't intend to go into great detail about blank selection or mounting methods in this series, but the sequence of operations is to mount the blank on the lathe, by either a faceplate or single screw chuck, holding to the face that will be the top of the bowl, turn the outside shape, including a recess to take the dovetail jaws of a chuck if you have one, and then reverse to hollow.

Must be secure

Whatever method you choose, it's vital the support is secure, particularly for your first few bowls, when errors are more likely. Bowls are only mounted on one face, whereas spindles are supported at both ends, so there is greater risk with bowls. Wear face protection, preferably in the form of an air-fed helmet or at least a face shield, at all times.

Always check that the blank toolrest won't hit the toolrest by rotating it by hand before starting the lathe. Also check that the lathe is on a slow speed at this stage. Avoid standing at right angles to the lathe in line with the blank, because experience has taught me that this is the preferred route for most bowls to escape.

The tool will move more easily across the toolrest if it's smooth, so spend a few minutes filing the top to remove any nicks.

In the photos the blank is smooth because I have turned off all the

Marking the centre in pencil.

irregularities, for cosmetic reasons. Normally I leave the sides rough, true up the base and work from the flat base around to the sides.

The part of the edge that cuts is marked with a felt-tip pen.

The toolrest's position depends on your height, the height of the lathe and how the tool will be used. Positioning will eventually become second nature, but to work it out I suggest you first mark the centre of the blank with a pencil while the wood is rotating.

You will be cutting from the centre outwards, so the part of the edge that will be cutting will be just to the right of the nose looking from underneath. If you raise and lower the toolrest with the tool on the rest until this part of the edge touches the centre spot with the bevel flat on the surface of the wood, the toolrest will be correctly positioned.

The reason I suggest cutting from inside to out is that this means you start the cut with the tool in contact with the wood.

I normally cut from outside in, because centrifugal force is trying to push the tool outwards and it's easier to control the tool working against this force. But beginners sometimes have a problem with this, because the tool has to be lined up in the correct cutting position before meeting wood, and if the edge is uneven the first contact between tool and timber is a little bouncy.

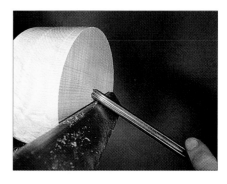

Positioning the toolrest.

Grain direction has no bearing on the matter because if the blank is cut from a plank in the normal way the grain is running at right angles to the lathe axis and the tool is working on side grain.

With the toolrest in the correct position, the gouge will have its flute (the channel) pointing to the left and the

Top view of cut. Note how my right hand is on the toolrest in this photo, whereas in the others it's my left. My thumb is on the tool and knuckles on the rest.

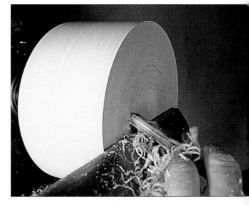

Side view of cut.

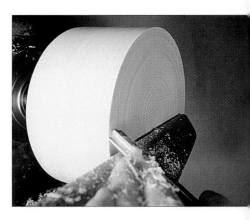

Side view of cut as it nears the edge.

angle in front of the gouge will be larger than the angle behind it.

Before starting the lathe check the speed, which should be slow to start with (I'd choose 790rpm). With the tool off the rest, you can now press the start button.

Place the tool on the rest and hold it there with one hand. Just because you're right-handed does not mean you have to use your left hand on the toolrest. Both hands work in turning, and you should be prepared to use either hand on the rest, whichever is most convenient.

Variable grip

The grip used largely depends on the shape of your hands and how flexible your fingers are. The role of the toolrest hand is to maintain contact between the tool and the rest and to work in opposition to the other hand. The bottom hand pushes the tool and rotates the handle, while the rest hand modifies these impulses.

I like to have two fingers on top of the tool and two in contact with the rest, but you may prefer to hold the tool with the thumb on the tool and the knuckles on the toolrest.

I don't like to see students wrapping their fingers around the tool and holding on with white knuckles, because this does not allow fine

adjustments to be made to the angle of cut.

When you become experienced and are hogging out the middle of a bowl you can use a grip like this, but early in your career it's more important to be responsive to the wood.

The bottom hand does need to be wrapped around the tool and any rolling required is done by the wrist. Control of the sideways movement comes from holding the end of the handle against the body and rocking the body from side to side. In other words, when cutting from right to left the weight of the body should start on the right foot and be gradually transferred to the left.

Tool position

First work out the position of the tool on the rest as above and then move your body up to the tool handle, until your right side is in contact with it. If you put your weight on your right leg at this point you can then lean to the left without losing your balance. Big, heavy boots also help!

With the tool on the rest, but not touching the work, move the tool towards the surface. If the bevel rubs firmly on the wood then the tool will only cut a very thin sliver at best, so the tip needs to be lowered until the

edge really bites when the tool can be moved across the surface.

Once the tool is cutting a nice shaving, the angle at which it is being held must be maintained across the base, or you will not produce a flat surface. The tool tip must move at the same speed as the end of the handle.

The recess can be hollowed with a bowl gouge and then made the correct size with a square-ended scraper.

When you reach the edge of the blank, try to keep the tool going in the same line as it was when rubbing on the wood, or it will vibrate on the ragged surface, which can be alarming. If it goes towards the lathe at this point it's a sure sign that you are pressing the tool against the wood rather than down on the rest.

The first cuts are done to clean up the surface so you can see if any cracks are hidden by the dirt and rough saw marks. There are usually irregularities in the surface which will cause the tool to bounce. If you press the tool hard against the wood you will make them worse, so the rest hand should press down on the tool-rest not towards the wood.

Concave base

As you clean up the bottom, remember the base will need to be slightly concave so that the base of the bowl will sit on a surface without rocking. This can be done by taking more off the centre of the base than the edges during these first cuts.

When you are satisfied the base is free from faults and concave, mark the size of the recess for dovetail jaws

Side view of square-ended scraper

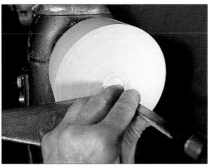

The square-ended scraper in use.

Using the square-ended scraper in the recess.

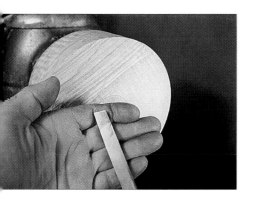

Plan view of the square-ended scraper.

in the base with one of the points of a pair of dividers while the wood is rotating. If you only have a faceplate for remounting you will need to mark the centre in pencil and describe a circle for the plate's diameter.

A dovetail recess can be hollowed with the bowl gouge and made the correct size with a square-ended scraper. If you don't want to buy a 13mm(½in) scraper you can easily modify an old chisel.

The end of the scraper is ground to the angle of the dovetail jaws so that when the end is parallel with the flat

base of the recess the side of the recess will be the correct angle.

The left side of the tool is also ground, so that the top is wider than the bottom, to prevent the bottom edge fouling the wall of the recess.

It's less likely to catch if used pointing down, so the toolrest should be raised so that when the edge cuts the centre of the recess the end of the handle is higher than the cutting edge.

The best way to make the bottom flat is to start with the right-hand end of the edge lined up with the centre of the recess and the edge parallel with the bottom. Push the tool towards the wood and the left-hand edge will make a small step by the time the right hand edge contacts the wood.

Withdraw the tool and move it 5mm (³⁄₁₆in) to the left before repeating the operation. Continue until you reach the line marking the diameter of the recess.

At this point the tool should be pushed diagonally, so that it produces

an overhang. To remove the last vestiges of steps in the recess the edge can be moved from side to side. You are now ready to shape the outside, which I'll describe next month. ∎

Better bowls
Part Two

Shaping the outside

When you've trued up the bottom of a bowl and catered for the remounting, it's a good time to offer up your chuck to check it will fit the recess, or the faceplate the drawn circle.

If the hole for the chuck is too small the solution is easy, but if it is too large you either lose a few millimetres off the depth of the bowl and make a new recess or you insert a circle of wood or MDF, glue it in place and use a compression fit chuck on the resultant spigot.

Once you are satisfied on this count, you can work out how big you should make the base. For a bowl of 150mm (6in) diameter such as this I like the base to be about 75mm (3in) in diameter. Much smaller and the bowl looks unstable, but much bigger and it looks clumpy.

If, however, the smallest jaws for your chuck are 63mm (2½in) you will need to leave 13mm (½in) either side of the recess to support the expansive pressure of the jaws which will necessitate a base of 88mm (3½ins). The recess in the photos is 44mm (1¾ins) so the base can be just under 74mm (3in). The toolrest can stay across the bottom because the rounding process will start with the bevel resting on the flat surface of the base.

The gouge is used as it was on the base, with the flute pointing in the direction of cut and cutting being done with the part of the edge just to the left of the nose when looking down on the flute (photo 1).

I like to start near the corner with the bevel flat on the base and swing the tool round to round off the corner keeping the bevel near the surface of

the wood as I go. Each subsequent cut starts further to the right and ends further up the side (photo 2).

Cutting in this direction is cutting with the grain, because the fibres you

Photo 2. **Rounding the sides.**

are cutting are supported by the fibres underneath. If you tried to turn in the opposite direction it would be a lot harder, the finish would be bad and the grain at the end of the cut (the bottom of the bowl) would tend to chip out.

At this point you have to commit yourself to a design. The photos show a typical Regester shape, which I like to think of as a beautiful curve, a shape I admire in all sorts of contexts and which I'm still trying to perfect in every bowl.

It looks easy to do because of the years of practice I have put in and, as the shape flows, so does the tool in the formation.

Photo 1. **Starting to round the corner.**

I've watched many students try to reproduce this shape and at first was surprised they found it so hard to do. Now I'm surprised when they succeed.

It's a good idea to copy a shape like this when you are learning, but when you gain more experience you will probably find it more satisfying to develop a shape of your own.

The shape is created by the swing of the tool (see photos 3, 4 and 5). Needless to say I am not recommending that you do it one handed, I am simply showing the arc the tool has to go through to make the shape and keep the bevel supporting the cut all the way.

Photo 3. **The start of the tool action when creating a curve.**

Photo 4. **The middle section...**

Photo 5. **...The conclusion.**

The grip of the tool pressed against the body and the transfer of the body weight from right foot to left, is shown in photos 6 and 7.

Notice how the toolrest has been moved round to reduce the overhang of the tool which reduces the amount of flexing between the toolrest and the tip. Stop the lathe when adjusting the toolrest, to avoid getting your fingers trapped between rest and timber.

Co-ordinating the movement of the tool across the surface of the bowl while keeping the cutting angle correct, is the most difficult aspect of turning.

If the edge moves faster than the handle, the bevel gets too close to the surface and the shavings become thinner. This means you don't remove enough timber. But if you press the bevel too hard against the wood you will compress the grain and get chatter lines, which you feel as vibration before you see them.

The damage

When you stop to inspect the damage you will see that the surface of the wood is shiny where the bevel has been rubbing, and there will be diagonal ridges.

The answer is to move the handle faster than you did before, but invariably you over-compensate and dig a furrow.

Getting this bit right requires cheap timber to waste and patience or bloody mindedness. You simply have to practise and try to remember what you did right when it goes right and what went wrong when it doesn't.

You can save yourself a lot of time by getting a good tutor to show you where you are going wrong. They will probably spot the fault at once, and the answer will probably be just a slight adjustment to your action. This will make all the difference, but takes ages to work out for yourself.

The subtle differences between doing it right or wrong are almost impossible to convey in the written word, but I'm doing my best.

During the shaping, keep stopping to see what you've done. Inspect the surface of the wood for faults such as

Photo 6. **The tool is pressed against the body and the body weight is transferred from the right foot...**

Photo 7...**to the left foot.**

cracks or stains, which you may want to turn away.

You may be tempted (as we all are) to change your intended shape to cater for the flaws you wish to avoid. Think carefully before doing this. Expediency is not a good design consultant and my reject pile contains several naff-shaped compromises that ought never to see the market place.

On the other hand, this process occasionally throws up a good shape you would never have thought of.

Photo 8. **The finish achieved by the straight-across gouge, the flute pointing in the direction of the cut**.

it will only get worse." But listen hard and you will hear me saying: "If you do not try to get a good finish from the tool despite the risk of messing up you will never improve."

When you've tried the sharp tool and fine cut you may want to see if using the tool differently will improve things. This way requires some skill and perhaps you should only try it if you have achieved a smooth action using the tool 'properly'.

Using a back cut as in photos 9 and 10 (and done in that order) has the advantage of using the other side of the tool to that which you used for roughing out, which should mean it will still be sharp.

The trick is to be able to tell the good from the bad, and the best way to find out is to put it to one side and look at it later.

Photo 8 shows the finished shape achieved with the gouge used as described. The ash is highly figured and wet, so the grain has risen towards the top and there are lines left by the tool. This is the usual result of using the tool in this way, because it has been cutting with a tightly-curved edge which is bound to leave a grooved surface.

Photo 9. **The start of the back cut....**

Groovy

The tool has also been used for the whole process of roughing down the bowl without sharpening, so it has lost its keenness. If your action is not as smooth as mine it will leave even more-obvious grooves.

Now, if the bowl is to be left to dry this surface is acceptable, but if you want to practise techniques that will be used to produce a finished bowl, you should aim to produce a better finish from the tool. This is done by using a sharp tool and taking fine cuts, so put a sharp edge on the tool and use it in the same way as before to see how good a finish you can get.

You will say to yourself: "That's as good as it gets and if I mess around

Photo 10 ....**nearing the end of the back cut**.

movement may be quite slow – he just does no more of these than he needs to.

Aim for a smooth overall shape with no rough patches of grain, because large ridges and hollows and picked-up grain take ages to remove by sanding. A succession of small ridges on a usually smooth curve present less of a problem.

Photo 11 shows the finish obtained by using the back cut, having sharpened the gouge on the benchgrinder. The finish is better than that seen in photo 8, although it may not be visible here.

I also made the cut after sharpening the tool to perfection on the Tormek, and the results are shown in photo 12. It did not make enough difference to warrant the extra effort – but it felt good.

At this stage you would take the blank off the lathe if you were practising or just roughing out. If you are going for the finished article with dry wood, you can sand and finish. ■

Photo 11. **The finish from the back cut sharpened on the benchgrinder.**

It also uses the side of the tool, which is a short straight edge rather than a curve, so less likely to leave grooves.

The downside is that it's more difficult to control than the usual way, and if you allow the gap between bevel and wood to get too big you will have a mighty dig-in.

When doing a fine cut it's important to make the edge pass over the surface, taking a thin cut all the way. You can tell the thickness of the cut by the size of the ridge formed at the tool tip, and the trick is to keep this the same all the way over the surface.

It's not easy but, with practice, you can make a surface smooth with one or two passes of the tool. It is better to do one cut like this slowly and in a controlled way, than several fast strokes which leave a rough surface. If you watch a professional at work you may think that he works quickly because he will produce a finished item at speed. But if you look more closely you will probably see that each

Photo 12. **The finish from back cut sharpened on Tormek.**

Better bowls
Part Three

Hollowing bowls with a straight-across ground gouge

When you are satisfied with the outside shape of your bowl, remove it from the lathe and remount it with the top exposed, using your favourite method.

If you plan to use a chuck with expanding jaws it's essential to put the chuck on the lathe and then the bowl on the chuck.

Tighten the chuck just enough to hold the bowl, so you can check its concentricity by rotating it by hand and sighting against a marker such as a spot on the wall, or even check it in relation to the toolrest.

Some chucks (particularly those that rely on elastic bands to hold the jaws in place) need a push with the flat of the hand to seat the jaws in the recess. Only tighten them when you are satisfied the bowl is centred.

Trouble

If you expand the jaws firmly into the recess and then find the bowl is not concentric you will be in trouble, because the jaws distort the recess.

Before starting to hollow, decide what you want to achieve. Most people like the inside of any sort of bowl – wood, pottery or metal – to mirror the outside. In other words, to have an even wall thickness.

Some variation is desirable, such as a slight overhang at the rim which casts a shadow and makes the bowl look deeper. But a rim of 13mm (½in) and a bottom of 25mm (1in) would

feel heavier than it looked, which can be unsettling. Random variations in wall thickness, and especially a thick bottom, speak more of a lack of technical proficiency than an individual approach to turning design.

It's a good design principle that if you are going for the unusual, make it radically different from the norm, so it looks intentional. So, if you want to make a bowl with an inside shape different to that of the outside, make it vary a lot.

Shaping

If you want to make a bowl with an even wall thickness, the way to achieve this is not so much by regular checking with callipers, but by picturing in your mind the outside shape and trying to emulate it as you hollow.

Don't just hack out the inside as best you can and then make the shape right. Let your first cut follow the shape and continue in this way. Then the inside shape will emerge smooth, without too many ridges and furrows.

The first job after the bowl has been mounted is to true up the top just as you trued up the bottom. Only when you have removed the old surface can you be sure there are no faults in the wood, and only when you have made the top level can you accurately measure the depth and work out how deep you can hollow.

The cut is made exactly as it was on the base, with the gouge cutting

Photo 1 **Truing the top of the bowl.**

from the centre outwards and the flute pointing in the direction of cut (photo 1). When the top is flat, measure the depth by placing one ruler

Photo 2 **Inserting a depth gouge.**

across the base and a second ruler at right angles to that (on the side of the bowl), so that you measure from the base to the top edge.

The depth you can hollow to is the total depth minus the length of the screws plus 6mm (¼in), if using a faceplate. If using a chuck, it's to the depth of the recess plus 13mm (½in). This will give a margin for error should you make a mistake, but aim eventually to make the bottom less thick than this.

Drill a hole of this depth down the centre of the blank, using either a straight narrow carving gouge (photo 2), or a drill bit in a Jacob's chuck, which you can hold by hand provided you push it in straight. I make a funnel opening at the top of the hole, because I use my thumb as a depth stop and this allows any escaping steam to dissipate before it hits my thumbnail.

When hollowing, you will see this hole and when it disappears you will know you have nearly reached the bottom of the inside. As a bonus you will avoid producing a nipple in the bottom of the bowl which can be very difficult to remove.

Wall thickness

The next step is to decide how thick you want the walls. If there's a chance your bowl will be good enough to leave to dry, then the width of the walls should be about 10% of the bowl's width. If you are using dry wood then it is just a matter of taste.

Beginners should make a groove where the inside of the rim will be, so that if the tool should skate across the surface out of control it will not damage the rim. You can use the square-ended scraper with which you made the recess (photo 3), or the point of a skew chisel, provided you lay it on its side on the toolrest.

Hollowing must be done from the outside towards the middle, because this is working with the grain. You must cut so that the fibres you are cutting are supported by those underneath, or you'll find it hard work and it will only produce a very rough surface. It is also working

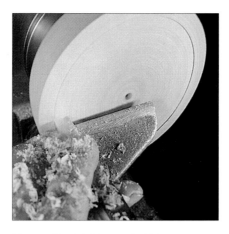

Photo 3 **Establishing wall thickness stop cut, with the square scraper.**

against the natural tendency of the rotation to throw the tool outwards, and this makes the tool easier to control.

To make the shape of the inside conform with the outside, I like to

Photo 4 **Starting to hollow near the centre.**

Photo 5 **Halfway through the hollowing, showing the line in front of the cut which the bevel must relate to.**

Photo 6 **The arc of the cut – entry angle....**

Photo 7 **....Highest point....**

Photo 8 **....Cutting through the centre.**

start cutting from near the centre (photo 4) making the hollow both deeper and wider with each cut until I reach the edge (photo 5). This photo clearly shows how the tool is cutting with the part of the edge that is just under the nose.

The bevel is close to the side of the bowl to give the edge support, but it's

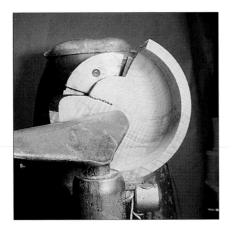

Photo 9 **Cut-away bowl, showing the arc of the cut in black.**

also close just under the point where it is cutting. This can only be achieved if the tool is pointed upwards as it goes inwards and the flute pointed to the right at about 2 o'clock on the dial. The tool should describe an arc while it enters, as shown in photos 6, 7 and 8, taken from a position level with the centre of the lathe. This is the bulk-removal cut, when the quality of the surface left by the tool is not important.

I cut away part of the bowl and blackened the arc of cut (see photo 9).

Photo 10 **The view from top of entry point....**

When viewed from the top, as in photos 10,11, 12 and 13, you can see how the tool can go over the whole surface of the inside with the bevel in contact to give a good finish from the tool when it is sharp.

Note how the toolrest is angled inside the bowl to give the closest

Photo 11 **....Halfway through the cut....**

Photo 12 **....Nearing the centre....**

possible support, and how the tool starts off at right angles to the rest and finishes nearly parallel to it.

This means the tool handle has passed through a 90° arc, and in this shape of bowl ends with the shaft nearly rubbing the rim of the bowl.

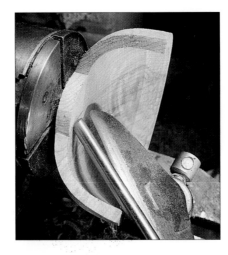

Photo 13 **....Cutting through the centre, with the tool nearly parallel to the toolrest**.

It contrasts with photo 8 where the end of the cut has the tool still almost at right angles to the toolrest as in photo 11. The reason for the difference is that when removing timber at speed the bevel does not need to remain in such close contact.

The cut should always end with the cutting edge passing through the exact centre of the bowl, otherwise you will leave a raised area at this point. If you have reached the maximum depth of the bowl this cut should be very thin at this point, in other words feathered off.

As a turner, you need to become skilled enough to remove timber precisely where you want, and this includes being able to increase and decrease the depth of cut at will while traversing a surface.

The latter is not done by the degree of pressure on the tool but by altering the distance between the bevel and the surface of the wood. If the bevel is close to the wood you can only achieve a shallow cut, but if you raise the bevel the depth increases.

Rough surface

If you have a hand plane it is like pushing the blade of a plane further through the slot. As you increase the blade's projection, you remove more wood but leave a rougher surface, until you get to the point where the blade projects so far the wood is ripped. So, in turning, the bevel can be raised to remove more wood, but the grain will tear out.

When the extreme is reached with the plane it grinds to a halt, because the shoe stops the blade tunnelling into the wood. But with a turning tool there is no shoe, so the tool burrows into the timber and either gets jammed or catches.

Another similarity is that when using a plane there is a tendency to believe that the blade is not removing shavings because it is not projecting enough, when the real reason is that the blade is not sharp.

Remove the inevitable ridges and furrows on the inside of a bowl by first locating the exact position of a raised area with your finger tips.

If you can't relocate this area when you start the lathe you can mark it with a pencil. Then start the lathe and hold the tool in its cutting position, lightly against the inside of the bowl before the ridge, but with the bevel rubbing and the edge not in contact.

If you move the tool handle so the tool moves towards the ridge and the edge slowly begins to bite, you should feel when you reach the ridge. Keep the tool in line and the depth of cut should increase as you climb the ridge and decrease as you descend the other side.

Good finish

With a really sharp gouge it's possible, with practice, to get a good finish from the tool with most types of wood. You should aim to remove areas of rough grain which often show up in two sections where the grain is short. If you have difficulty achieving this, it often helps to dampen the fibres with water or finishing oil (depending on which is compatible with the finish).

This softens them, and they can be cut instead of bending away from the edge of the tool. Rough grain takes a long time to sand away, but a series of small ridges on the surface can soon be removed with abrasives.

If I cannot achieve a good finish from the gouge, I use a half-round scraper for the final cut (photo 14). I use a converted carbon steel skew

chisel, 50mm wide x 8mm thick (2 x ⁵⁄₁₆in), bought ages ago from Robert Sorby. It's no longer listed in their catalogue, but Henry Taylor still make such a tool.

This tool needs to be as heavy and thick as possible to give stability on the toolrest and avoid any flexing due to the overhang which can occur in deep bowls, but the maximum size usually listed of 38mm (1½in) is adequate for most purposes.

I use the tool to take off the merest slivers of wood from inside the bowl. I've always thought the idea of using the burr thrown up by sharpening on the bench grinder to make little sense, because it will last only a short time when held against rotating wood, and raising a burr is so imprecise a science that it's hard to achieve consistency. Having now seen the ragged edge of such a burr through a microscope, I feel thoroughly vindicated.

Sharp edge

I've always preferred to use a sharp edge on my scrapers and have achieved very good results using this method. I've used a burr, sometimes with good results, but have found the cut to be more snatchy, and frequent sharpening to be required.

The secret of using a sharp scraper is to make the bevel longer than is usual. I prefer 50° and find a longer bevel can result in the tool having a smaller area of flat available to sit on the toolrest, which can cause instability. This is especially noticeable in small scrapers.

I sharpen the scraper on the Tormek system flat table and remove any burr by rubbing the top face on the side of the wheel. If you don't have a Tormek, the same effect can be achieved by sharpening on a benchgrinder and honing the top with a slipstone or diamond file.

Snatches

I had occasional snatches with a scraper until I realised this was caused by the tool not moving smoothly across the toolrest. The toolrest was smooth, so the problem was not caused by dents in its surface.

I felt the scraper's underside and found a burr had developed which was catching on the rest and offering different amounts of resistance, depending on the alignment. Now I hone the top and bottom of the scraper when I sharpen, and have few catches.

I use the scraper with the toolrest higher than when using a gouge, so that when cutting through the centre of the bowl the tool is pointing downwards by a few degrees. Snatches with a scraper happen more often on the side of bowls where end grain is encountered than in the bottom, and you need to go very gently with the tool.

Some students have an involuntary reflex to rotate the tool handle when moving the tool. This results in the bottom face lifting off the rest on the side nearest the wood. When contact with the wood is made, the tool is slammed down on the toolrest and you get a catch.

Next month, I'll discuss the advantages of using a ground-back gouge and how to sharpen it. ■

Photo 14
The final cut with the scraper

Better bowls
Part Four

The ground-back bowl gouge

My previous articles on bowl turning have shown the use of the bowl gouge with a straight-across grind, as it's usually supplied. I wanted to show that it is possible to turn a bowl of that design without modifying the tool.

Most beginners find it difficult enough to sharpen the gouge as supplied and to learn how to use it that way, without tackling tool modification as well.

The only ground-back gouge on the market I know of is the David Ellsworth gouge, made by Crown Tools. This is an excellent tool, but subtly different to the shape of mine and used in a different way.

The shape is a good introduction to the advantages of this profile, but for those who wish to modify a straight-across grind I'll describe how to.

Cheapest

The cheapest and most common way of sharpening woodturning tools is the bog-standard benchgrinder with fitted toolrest. This should be fitted with aluminium oxide wheels for high speed steel, and I recommend one 60 grit for tool modification and a 100 grit for sharpening.

The alternative is a water-cooled grinder such as the Tormek, which uses a bigger grind wheel that rotates at a slow speed and passes through a water trough.

It avoids the overheating problem and produces a beautiful sharp edge, but it takes a long time to radically alter tool shapes and costs a lot more than a benchgrinder.

Toolrests are always provided on benchgrinders, usually being a flat platform. The Tormek is fitted with a bar which can be used as a toolrest or a support for a range of rests and jigs, according to your needs.

I've reviewed the Tormek system elsewhere so will confine myself to passing mentions of its virtues.

Problem

The problem with the flat toolrest standard on most benchgrinders is that the angles required for the bevels are not right angles. So you must either learn to reproduce the angles free-hand like most professionals, which takes much time and practice, or buy a piece of kit which sets them for you.

The O'Donnell system I have reviewed previously is a system that comprises a table which can be adjusted to different angles by a series of notches on the stem. It's adjustable for the wear of the wheel, but only to the extent of a 25mm (1in) reduction in diameter.

Tobias Kaye's and the Wolverine system both have an adjustable table and a gouge jig. The Robert Sorby jig is just for fingernail gouges and does not have a table.

Whatever bench grinder or system you use, it's vital to wear eye protection, because pieces of metal can come off the wheel at unpredictable angles and seriously damage an eye.

As you can see, my grinder is fitted with shields which are usually over the stone but have been lifted off to give clearer photos.

I have used the O'Donnell system to demonstrate non-jig grinding, but my remarks apply whatever platform you use.

Photo 1. **Ground back gouge.**

In photo 1, the gouge's ground-back edge slopes back from the nose at about 45°. To produce this profile, put the tool on the benchgrinder toolrest with the flute downwards so you can present the top of the tool to the wheel.

Grind it so you develop a straight line from the edge on top of the bevel at the nose to the flute of 45°. This produces a flat where an edge should be, so you then have to make a bevel up this line and a sharp edge all around the sides.

Most work needs to be done at the sides where the flat is widest, so I usually work on these areas alternately to avoid too much heat building up in the steel.

I like to keep an even bevel all the way round, with the grooves cut by the grind wheel at right angles to the edge, because I find this makes the tool easier to control.

To get this effect the edge should be parallel to the top edge of the wheels (horizontal). You can see this in photo 2, where I'm using the O'Donnell jig.

When you have created edges on both sides, the bevel should be carried all the way to the nose so that the edge is a smooth shape.

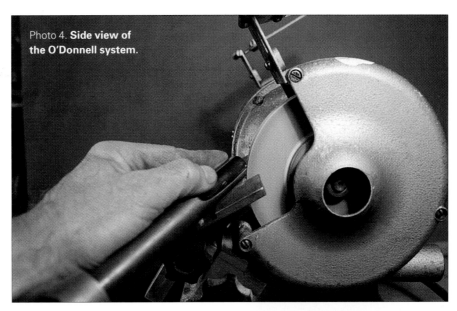

Photo 4. **Side view of the O'Donnell system.**

Photo 2. **O'Donnell system grinding side with edge horizontal.**

To do this you need to swing the tool round so that when the grinding starts on the right side of the tool (photo 2), the handle is pointing to the right. Photo 4 shows this from the side.

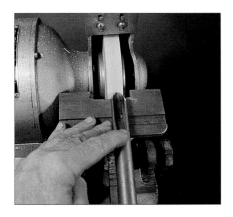

Photo 3. **O'Donnell system sharpening nose on.**

When grinding the nose, the handle is at right angles to the grinder and the nose is higher on the wheel (photos 3 and 5) and when the grinding finishes on the left side the tool is right over to the left.

This is, of course, easier to say than to do, and mastering a smooth motion with the tool is as hard as learning to turn with it.

Never press on the tool, but repeatedly check progress, marking the bevel with a felt-tip pen if you cannot see which parts you've ground.

If you need to remove more steel in one area than another, just spend a little longer at that point. You will know you have succeeded when there is a continuous bevel all the way around, a smooth profile and no light reflects from the edge.

Drastic profile alteration always leaves a burr inside the flute. A pass or two up and down the flute with the edge of a slipstone will remove most of this and leave a sharp cutting edge.

Several grinding jigs will help you to achieve this grind, including those from Tobias Kaye, Sorby and One-Way Wolverine grinding jigs and the special jig for the Tormek system.

All these jigs work in a similar way, in that you insert the gouge into a collar so it projects by a set amount. The gouge is held in place with a screw and the tool is moved

Photo 5. **O'Donnell system sharpening nose on.**

against the grind wheel and moved across the wheel in a pattern governed by a pre-set jig.

They all work well and enable you to get a consistent profile and bevel angle, provided you set them up with a fair idea of what you are aiming for and have followed the instructions. I'll make a few comments about each jig:

Tormek

This jig will only work with the Tormek system. It functions very efficiently, enabling you to produce a consistent shape, provided you've set it up correctly. You need to ensure the settings are the same each time to sharpen the tool.

I like to use a short length of 25mm (1in) diameter tube to measure the projection of the gouge through the tool holder. This jig cannot hold a gouge larger than 19mm (¾in).

The Tormek system has many advantages, but is slow at profile changing, so if you invest in a Tormek and want to save time, I suggest you also get an ordinary benchgrinder for this.

Tobias Kaye

To set up this jig you need to make the height of the centre of the grind wheels 250mm (10in) above the surface the jig rests on, which in my case meant that the grinder was then too high to comfortably use.

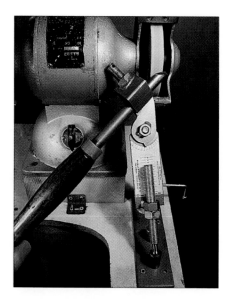

Photo 6. **Tobias Kaye sharpening jig.**

For most people, who have the grinder at table height, this will raise it to a more suitable height, and if I needed the jig I would saw three inches off my table legs.

You also need to cut out a specially-shaped board to stand the jig on and this has to project 125mm (5in) in front of the grinder.

Once set up the jig is simple to use, and gave me consistent results. Photo 6 shows the front view of sharpening the left side and photo 7 shows sharpening the nose.

Photo 7. **Tobias Kaye jig sharpening nose on.**

The table that fits on the same base allows adjustment of sharpening angles and also takes wheel wear into consideration. A guard stops the shaft of the table being fouled with the rubbish thrown off by the grinder.

One-Way

I needed no table modification for the One-Way system, but some grinders may have to be raised by about 25mm (1in).

The instructions recommend that a hole be drilled in a suitable piece of wood so that the projection of the gouge through the jig can be repeated whenever it is sharpened. I did this in the leg of my grinder stand (photo 8).

The One-Way Wolverine system includes a jig support arm, which projects in front of the grinder when in use and behind when not (photo 9).

If you don't want to have the platform or to use the vee arm for straight-across ground gouges, then it's possible to use the jig without the

Photo 8. **One-Way Wolverine jig setting projection of gouge through jig.**

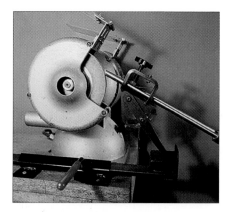

Photo 9. **The One-Way Wolverine jig, sharpening the nose of a gouge.**

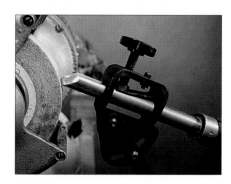

Photo 10. **Close up of the Wolverine jig, sharpening the nose of a gouge.**

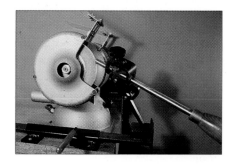

Photo 11. **The One-Way Wolverine jig sharpening the side of a gouge.**

support by making a stop on the table. Photo 10 shows sharpening the nose and photo 11, the side.

The Wolverine instructions are thorough and informative, enabling the user to get the best from their investment.

Sorby

The Sorby system is only for ground-back gouges. It's basically a support for a jig produced in close cooperation with Tormek. Similar to the ones supplied for use with Sorby's water-cooled grinder, it has the advantage of a brass knob which ensures the gouge is positioned square in the jig.

This system was very easy to install and use. I only had to build a platform for it, because my ancient grinder has such a tall base.

Photo 14. **Side view of the Sorby jig.**

Photo 12. **Sorby jig, sharpening the right side of a gouge.**

Photo 13. **The Sorby jig sharpening nose on.**

All these jigs enabled me to obtain a consistent profile and bevel, and I'm sure any one of them would give years of accurate gouge sharpening.

They are all different, and the one you plump for must depend on your precise needs. If you just want a simple jig, then the Sorby system is clearly the cheapest and did an excellent job, although if you wish to use a toolrest on the same stone it may not be possible to have both options open at once.

If you want a platform as well, then both Tobias Kaye's and the Wolverine are perfectly efficient, but my vote would go to the former for ease of use and price. ∎

Suppliers

David Ellsworth signature gouge:
Crown Tools, Excelsior Works,
Burnt Tree Lane, Sheffield S3 7EX.
Tel: 0114 272 3366. Fax: 0114 272 5252.

Tobias Kaye:
10 Lower Dean, Buckfastleigh,
Devon TQ11 OLS.
Tel/Fax: 01364 642 837.

One-Way Wolverine:
Craft Supplies, The Mill, Millers Dale,
Buxton, Derbyshire SK17 8SN.
Tel: 0800 146417. Fax 01298 872263.

Robert Sorby:
Athol Road, Sheffield S8 OPA.
Tel: 0114 225 0700. Fax: 0114 225 0710.

Tormek:
BriMarc Associates, 7-8 Ladbroke Park,
Warwick CV34 5AE.
Tel: 01926 493389. Fax: 01926 491357.

C & M O'Donnell:
Brough, Thurso, Caithness,
Scotland KW14 8YE.
Tel: 01847 851605. Fax: 01847 851793.

Better bowls
Part Five

Using a ground-back gouge

We change the shape of a tool to make it work better for the user. Turners working on their own learn to use a tool of a certain profile for one job, and change when faced with another. But those who belong to a woodturning club, visit woodworking shows, read books or turning magazines, see many different profiles.

They are tempted to try as many as possible without really understanding them or sticking with them long enough to become proficient.

My advice is to learn to use a tool of basic shape and only try to modify it when you have fully understood its purpose. If the new shape works, stick with it. If it doesn't, try another.

No one tool shape will make you a good turner overnight, but it may help after practising with it.

Main advantage

The main advantage of the ground back profile over the straight across grind is that the cutting edge is extended around the sides of the tool. This makes it safer, because it removes the corners which could catch.

It also increases the cutting edge, enabling wider shavings to be removed, and gives more choice of how to present the tool to the work.

It decreases the radius of the nose, too, enabling the tool to penetrate the tight curves inside a bowl while still keeping bevel support.

Richard Raffan introduced me to this profile in the early 1980s, but it

Photo 1. **Cutting across the bottom of the work, using the side of the gouge.**

was not until I saw David Ellsworth demonstrate it at the first Loughborough seminar seven years later, that I really understood its potential.

I adopted it after that, and thought I was using the same profile as David. But when I caught up with him in France 10 years later, I found we were sharpening it in subtly different ways and using the tool very differently.

I have now had a chance to try out the Ellsworth Signature Gouge produced by Crown Tools and can see even more clearly where we differed.

It's a big advantage to be able to buy a tool ready sharpened to this profile, but difficult to replicate the shape when sharpening. The instructions' lack of illustration don't help.

The main difference between sharpening this tool and mine, is that the grooves left by the grinder do not all run at right angles to the edge. Instead of keeping the edge parallel to the grinder's axis, the tool should go up the stone as you grind along the sides.

This can be done on the Tormek, using the fingernail jig by setting the jig angle at four and the height of the universal support at 47mm (about 1¾in) with the standard projection through the jig of 65mm (2⅝in).

The best way to learn how to use any profile is take lessons from someone who can show you how to grind and use their variant. The next best option is to grind it from written instructions, or a video.

Sharpening comparison

Last month I made the case for radically changing a profile with a bulk-standard bench grinder rather than a water-cooled one, because it's faster. What I didn't mention is that the sharpness of the edge produced by a water-cooled system such as the Tormek has no competition.

The first cut with a tool sharpened in this way on a jig, is a revelation in terms of smoothness and finish. View the edge through a microscope and

Photo 2. **Rounding the outside of the bowl.**

you will see you get a mountain range with a bench grinder, compared with the Tormek's smooth plain.

You need to press the tool hard onto the wheel to get a good bevel on a Tormek, and this is not possible freehand. I can sharpen most tools on the table, but gouges need the jig, which gives total control and repeatability.

If tool sharpness is the only consideration, a Tormek is a must, and this remains my opinion if time is not a factor. But life is not that simple.

The bottom line for professionals has to be an overall saving in time, though evaluating this is difficult without extensive research.

Without an objective and repeatable method, factors such as personal prejudice and the natural human tendency to compensate for tool wear by extra pressure on the tool affect results.

The table below is a balance sheet:

Photo 3. **Making a finishing cut with the side of the tool.**

cut twenty-four 300 x 300 x 100mm (12 x 12 x 4in) blanks and roughed out the outsides so they were all of the same shape and size. I also cut recesses, so they could be mounted on a four-jaw chuck.

I sharpened my 22mm (⅞in) gouge on a Tormek and started hollowing them. I'd finished 11 before the tool was too blunt to continue.

Photo 4. **The finish obtained from a Tormek-sharpened tool.**

2. The tool sharpened on a bench grinder performs as well as the Tormek sharpened for bulk removal for the first few minutes, but then performance falls off fairly quickly, whereas the Tormek's performance tapers off more slowly.
3. The time taken sharpening will probably only affect the professional

user, and will be made up for in the sharpness of the edge and the consistency of profile. The time taken would be reduced if the tool did not tend to rotate in the jig, as this affects the symmetry of the bevel produced.

Sorby have solved this problem by including a bronze alignment nut, which sits on top of the flute, and makes their jig quicker to use. With such a wheel in place I sharpened a blunt gouge on both the Sorby and Tormek systems jigs in 50 seconds.

Put right

I told BriMarc, who distribute the Tormek, about this and they have agreed to include the nut with gouge jigs as soon as possible, together with a set of instructions, for if the gouge is clamped in wrongly, it can be very difficult to remove. If any reader would like one of these wheels to use in their jig, BriMarc will send one free on receipt of a stamped addressed envelope.
4. Price – a cheap bench grinder is unlikely to last as long as a Tormek. Even some of the more expensive bench grinders can take a long time to get up to speed, which affects their efficiency.

Regarding the price difference between the two Tormeks, the 2004

	TORMEK 1204	TORMEK 2004	BENCHGRINDER
Outlay (inc VAT)	£162.50	£285.50	£40.00
Spare wheel (inc VAT)	£46.44*	£85.19*	£18.00
Time taken to sharpen		1min 12secs	30secs

* These wheels last a lot longer than wheels on bench grinders, and their extra width makes them much better for sharpening other blades such as plane irons.

The time in the table was for sharpening one particular gouge that had been previously sharpened by the same method, so in the case of the Tormek the jig was already set up and the universal arm was in the correct position. In each test the tool was blunt and needed only a couple of passes over the wheel to become sharp again.

The timing was not to the nearest part of a second, because I didn't think such accuracy was needed. I'd expect there to be a wide variation in times, depending on the user's skill.

I did a small experiment when roughing out wet ash salad bowls. I

When I sharpened the tool on a bench grinder, using the Tobias Kaye jig, I hollowed nine before needing to sharpen.

I felt this was fairly objective, because I only stopped when the tool was too blunt to carry on and would have sharpened earlier for greater efficiency. But I can't rule out the possibility that I may have been prejudiced by knowing which sharpening method was used. The differences between the two methods are:
1. The Tormek gives a sharper edge than a bench grinder immediately off the wheel, and is therefore better for very fine finishing cuts.

Photo 5

Photo 6

Photo 7

Photos 5 - 7. **The cutting arc of the ground back gouge**.

is worth the extra in terms of wheel width and diameter and its continuously rated motor. Several students told me they had the 1204 and wished they'd paid the extra for the 2004.

Ground back gouge use

When turning the bowl used to illustrate this series, I did most of the work with a straight across ground bowl gouge. But I also took photos of a ground back gouge on the same bowl to show the differences in use.

Photo 1 shows how the bottom of a bowl can be made flat using the side of the tool, cutting from inside to out. This cut can be very fine and produce a smooth finish if the bevel is almost rubbing on the surface – if it's too far away the dig-in is horrific.

I use the tool for shaping the outside of a bowl with the flute pointing in the direction of cut like a straight across ground gouge (photo 2). To get a very smooth finish I use the side of the tool (photo 3). The finish obtained by the tool having been sharpened with a Tormek can be seen in photo 4.

Different angle

Because the bevel is a different shape, the angle at which the tool is held is different to that used when shaping the outside with a straight across grind. Photos 5,6 and 7 show the arc the tool passes through, but is not supposed to suggest that this be done one-handed.

The big advantage of the ground back profile is on the inside of a bowl,

where the shape allows the tool to be used with bevel support all around the cut. This can be seen in photos 8, 9 and 10.

It also allows the tool rest support to be closer to the end of the tool, giving more control. When hollowing the inside of the bowl, it's possible to take a very wide cut using the longer bevel. This makes bulk removal much quicker.

A problem area concerning tool control is the entry at the rim, where the gouge seems to want to shoot across the top, leaving an unsightly ragged effect.

I suffered this for years, and it seemed to be mainly a matter of chance whether it happened or not. On days when it went wrong it got worse the harder I tried, which was vexing.

I assumed the secret of success lay in lining up the bevel so that the piece of bevel in view was parallel with the inside of the bowl, but often as I tried to be more precise about this the fault got worse.

Then I noticed it is not just the bevel parallel to the inside of the bowl that has to be lined up but also the bevel in front of the tool, the part you can't see. The cut is the shape of the part of the gouge edge cutting, and the support for the cutting edge is also curved.

Tool skate

When trying to line up the bevel and still suffering from the skates, I was raising the end of the handle ever higher, so lessening the support for the inside edge of the tool. Photo 11 shows the front edge support of the bevel and that the flute has to be pointing up at this point to achieve this.

As the tool is moved further inside it can be rolled over, so the flute is pointing in the direction of cut and there is no danger of the tool skating out of control if pressure is maintained.

In the photos, I've used a 10mm (⅜in) bowl gouge, because you can turn all but the largest or smallest of bowls with one of these.

When finishing a bowl you can achieve an extra fine cut simply by sharpening the tool. I prefer to use a 6mm (¼in) bowl gouge for finishing because, being a thinner section tool,

Photo 8

Photo 9

Photo 10

Photos 8 - 10. **The hollowing cut.**

it seems to have a finer edge, but I also keep it just for the finishing cut, so it stays sharp and I don't have to sharpen the larger gouge as often.

If I only used a Tormek for sharpening I would probably use the same size tool for rough work and for finishing,

so that I did not have to change the setting on the jig.

I do a finishing cut inside the bowl, working from outside to in with the gouge (see photos 8 and 9),the bevel in close support because that is working with the grain.

I get a better finish on the bottom of the bowl by using the right hand side of the tool and working from the centre outwards, but only as far as the

point where the sides curve upwards, as you soon get into trouble if you cut against the grain there.

If I don't get a good finish from the gouge, I resort to other methods, including a scraper (see my article on hollowing with a straight across gouge in issue 61).

I use both gouge profiles, but if I had to choose just one would go for the ground back shape. ■

Suppliers

David Ellsworth signature gouge:
Crown Tools, Excelsior Works,
Burnt Tree Lane, Sheffield S3 7EX.
Tel: 0114 272 3366. Fax: 0114 272 5252.

Tobias Kaye:
10 Lower Dean, Buckfastleigh,
Devon TQ11 OLS.
Tel/Fax: 01364 642 837.

Sorby sharpening jig: Robert Sorby,
Athol Road, Sheffield S8 OPA.
Tel: 0114 225 0700. Fax: 0114 225 0710.

Tormek:
BriMarc Associates, 7-8 Ladbroke Park,
Warwick CV34 5AE.
Tel: 01926 493389. Fax: 01926 491357.

Photo 11. **Hollowing cut, showing leading bevel rubbing.**

Better bowls
Part Six

Texturing a bowl

I like simple, elegant bowls made from beautiful woods such as olive ash, yew, burr oak, burr elm or burr chestnut. I've occasionally tried more elaborate shapes but, whether due to lack of talent or because they go against my inclinations, they have not always been successful.

Yes, I've spent many years striving for simple elegant forms, and don't expect an end to the search. But I admire the exciting avenues being explored by other woodturners over shapes, or embellishments such as carving or colouring.

I've been loath to follow the latter trend because I love the natural characteristics of wood and have no talent for colouring.

Jules Tattersall is one turner whose embellished work I have long admired. His demonstration at Warwick last year inspired me to try a similar approach of staining and surface texturing, using an Arbortech blade on an angle grinder.

Texturing with the Arbortech appealed to me because it is so fast. I used the black stain shown in the photos because black is a colour I can relate to.

Photo 1 shows an ash bowl, 200 x 200 x 100mm (8 x 8 x 4in) which I decorated using similar techniques to the English oak bowl 250 x 250 x 100mm (10 x 10 x 4in) in the other photos.

I roughed this from unseasoned timber and left it dry for several years. Plain oak is prone to splitting if drying is hurried, so I had not kilned this sample.

I re-turned the bowl on the Axminster four-jaw chuck 63mm (2½in) dovetail jaws and, having got to a good finish from the tool, sanded it with 80 grit cloth backed aluminium oxide abrasive to remove any rough grain.

I lightly torched the bowl to accentuate the grain, as plain oak tends to be rather boring. This was done in the open air, where there was no risk of setting fire to anything else.

I used a gas-powered blow torch. The trick is to keep the flame moving

Photo 2. **Carving the rim with an Arbortech Mini-carver.**

Photo 1. **Ash bowl (8 x 8 x 4in).**

Photo 3. **Carving inside with a Mini-carver.**

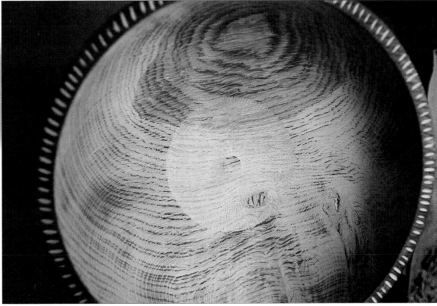

Photo 4. **The inner texturing before staining.**

over the surface of the wood until you have the right amount of charring. This highlights the annular rings and the medullary rays. It also transformed a few insignificant knots in my workpiece into attractive features.

I wanted the rim to be heavily charred and found it quite easy to do by keeping the flame playing over this area for longer than the rest. A wet cloth was kept handy, to stop any burning.

I replaced the bowl on the lathe and sanded it down to 320 grit, then textured the rim with the Arbortech Mini-carver on an angle grinder.

This is just like the original Arbortech, but with a smaller blade on a long arm. It's smaller size makes it easier to control, though it is still capable of doing major damage if you are not careful and don't wear safety gear such as a face shield and gloves.

I steadied the angle grinder's body on the tool rest and moved the blade onto the rim to make a small groove (photo 2).

The decoration did not need to be precise, so I judged the depth of cut by eye and then moved the bowl round so that the next groove would be made between 2 or 3mm (⁵⁄₆₄-⅛in) away. I tried to keep the blade constant at the same angle, but it did vary.

I wanted to decorate a circle in the middle, and as the long arm of the Mini-carver enables you to reach inside a bowl, I adapted one of Jules' techniques and used the Arbortech while the wood was rotating.

Jules tends to decorate the outside of bowls. Watching him demonstrate, I was puzzled at how he could go back and forth over an area and produce grooves that had a definite pattern rather than an area of random roughness.

He had not analysed the reasons for this, but it soon became apparent that the secret lies in holding the angle grinder so that your arms are locked against your body. You sway your body to and fro, so the arc of the tool is exactly repeated which gives regularity to the grooves.

I did this inside the bowl (photo 3) over an area about 10mm (4in) in diameter, trying to leave a raised point in the middle (photo 4).

The effect of this was not very definite at this stage, but I stained the area with some white vinegar in which I had been steeping some wire wool (photos 5 and 6) and knew that, when lightly sanded, the grooves would show up beautifully.

It did need a definite boundary, so I made a bead with a fluted parting tool (photo 7). This is not how the tool is intended to be used, but provided you are very careful and use it lightly with the flute pointing down, there should be no danger.

Sanding would blur the crisp edges needed, so the tool needs to be very sharp to get a good finish.

I rounded the raised central knob with a rectangular section skew chisel on its side (photo 8) and made a bead around it using the same method.

Photo 7. **Demarcation of the textured area with a fluted parting tool.**

Photo 5. **Staining the textured area.**

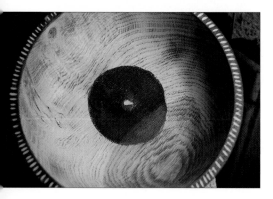

Photo 6. **The stained textured area.**

When satisfied with the smoothness of the wood, I coated it with a generous amount of Danish oil delivered by brush, left this to soak in for 20 minutes, and then started the lathe to buff the wood with some kitchen paper. The re-usable type is good for this job.

I repeated this application every 24 hours, until I had a finish just a bit shiny, but not glossy. I like the way the light catches the shiny bits between the charred parts.

The ash bowl shown was made by using similar techniques, but here I Arborteched the rim while it was rotating, then stained it and heavily charred an outside section. Later I cut grooves inside with an Arbortech while rotating it by hand.

In the advanced design class I took at Parnham College, Dorset, last year, I asked students to improve their bowls by expressing the idea of motion. Methods suggested included off-centre turning, texturing add-ons, colouring and carving.

My own expression of this can be seen in photo 9. It was made by re-turning a roughed out and dried oak bowl. I finished the inside and the rim smooth, but left an outside section which had warped in drying and appeared as a raised and rough-textured band.

Photo 10. **Handled bowls, (from right) box, walnut and apple.**

Photo 9.
**Reconstructed
oak bowl.**

Suppliers

RS200 and Sorby sharpening jig
supplied by: **Robert Sorby,
Athol Road, Sheffield S8 OPA.
Tel: 0114 2554231.**

**BCWA, 93 Parkway, Coxheath,
Maidstone, Kent ME17 4EX.**

Tormek and Arbortech Mini-carver
supplied by: **BriMarc Associates,
7-8 Ladbroke Park, Miller's Road,
Warwick CV34 5AE.
Tel: 01926 493389.**

Cylinder sander: **Carroll Sanders,
16-18 Factory Lane, Croydon, Surrey
CRO 3RL. Tel: 0181 781 1268.**

Woodturning courses:
**Parnham College, Beaminster,
Dorset DT8 3NA. Tel: 01308 862204.**

I stained this area with vinegar and wire wool and cut the whole thing into 10mm (⅜in) slices on the college's accurate bandsaw.

I played with the pieces to see what shapes they could make, and the best option was the heart shape shown, which reminds me of a boat. The pieces were glued with super glue.

Since the early 1980s I have experimented on and off with cutting up bowls after turning. This was inspired by a brief sighting of a Chinese spoon on television. My handled bowls (photo 10) are essentially hollow forms, 75 to 100mm high (3-4in) with 25mm (1in) openings.

I turn them using a combination of Bob Chapman inserts mounted in the BCWA shaft and then in the handle of a RS2000 tool, and scraper blades mounted on the RS2000 hooker.

I cut into them with a bandsaw and fine tune the shape with sanding discs held on the lathe and cylinder-mounted abrasives in a drill press.

If they are very thin they tend to shatter at the contact of a skip-tooth blade, in which case I shape with sanding discs.

I use dense, even-textured hardwoods such as box and walnut, and fruitwoods like cherry and apple. The wood does not have to be bone dry, as some warpage after finishing adds to the effect.

The 'spoon' bowls are difficult to make because the wall thickness has to be even and the inside needs to be sanded smooth. Any shortfalls are revealed by the cutting.

I've made subtle variations to their shape, but particularly like the way the rim seems to flow through the dimensions and how the inside becomes the outside.

The scope for bowl enhancement is limited only by your imagination, but I suggest you master simple bowls first and then try something more elaborate. That way you will have developed the skills to put your ideas into practice.

If you have an idea, go for it, having worked out on paper roughly what you want to do. But if you don't have any concrete ideas, choose a theme such as 'motion', or a line of poetry, and work out ways of expressing them. Viewers will not necessarily be able to see what you have tried to convey, but it does give you a starting point. ▪

Photo 8. **Turning the central knob with a skew chisel.**

Saw savvy

A look at saws, the bandsaw in particular

The author operating the bandsaw.

Before turning wood you first need to cut it roughly to size. Trees, sadly, do not grow with the turner in mind. Saws are best for this, be it a hand saw for cutting a branch to length to practise spindle turning, or a power saw to cut a bowl blank.

A saw is basically a row of teeth which pass and re-pass over wood to cut a groove. As with all woodworking equipment, it will only work efficiently if kept sharp. This means it must be treated with respect, because that which cuts wood is even better at cutting flesh. The best way to avoid damaging fingers is to keep them well away from the teeth.

Circular saw

A spindle turner could do much of his cutting with a hand saw, provided timber could be obtained in the correct cross-section. But he will sometimes want to cut wood along the grain, and this is hard work by hand.

The power tool most useful for this kind of work is a circular saw, either electric, saw bench, radial saw, or a drill attachment. The type you go for will depend on your budget and the tasks you have in mind.

A bowl turner needs to put roughly circular pieces of wood on the lathe, because converting a square blank to a circle using gouges

is hazardous and time consuming. The easiest option is to obtain ready-cut bowl blanks from local sawmills, turners' suppliers, or by mail order from firms advertising in this magazine.

Buying timber ready cut seems more expensive than buying the wood in plank form and converting it yourself, until you consider that buying a blank gives you what you

want and you don't have the expense of buying a saw.

If you buy a plank of seasoned hardwood and cut it into blanks you will find that the volume of the wood in the blanks may total only half of the volume of the plank. You will have to store the offcuts until you find a use for them or cannot move in your workshop and have to get rid of them.

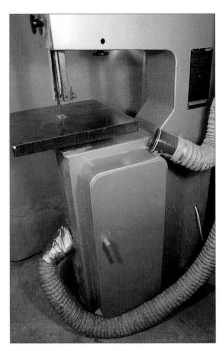

Dust extractor connections.

Buying ready cut blanks also has the advantage of enabling you to try different species of wood without committing you to buying a large quantity of just one. Please give some thought when buying wood to the affect the harvesting of that timber has had on the area where it grew. I try not to use imported hardwoods because I cannot be sure it has not been harvested at the expense of the lives or livelihood of some native tribe or flora and fauna.

The amount of wood I use is so small it does not make a difference to the continued existence of a given species of tree or ecosystem, and I know that tropical rain forests are destroyed not just for timber, but if everyone was conscious of the effect of their actions on the environment, our world would not be in the mess it is.

Sustainable

First try the woods growing in your area that you know can be harvested as part of a sustainable system. This may be ornamental trees that have outlived their useful lives, or temperate forest trees harvested as part of a commercial operation that is being renewed.

I've found British timbers to have such a variety of beautiful grain that I have no need of exotics of dubious provenance.

The most useful saw for a bowl turner is probably a chainsaw, because it will cut down your tree and convert it roughly to the required shape.

You should, however, go on a course to learn how to use it safely and maintain it correctly. Even a small electric chainsaw can inflict horrible injuries if misused.

If you want to cut lots of circular blanks the bandsaw is the best tool for the job, because the saw blade is very narrow, 3mm (⅛in) up to 19mm (¾in), enabling you to cut curves.

Which bandsaw?

There are makes and sizes of bandsaws on the market to cater for all budgets and needs. Mine is a Startrite 18-S-1 bought early in my career on the basis that it could cut the maximum size of blank I was using at the time.

I have no complaints about the quality of the saw, having worked it hard for 25 years and only had to replace bearings, blade guides and saw blades. But I would not advise a woodturner who makes a lot of bowls to buy a similar model.

I wish I'd bought a saw with a greater depth of cut and two band wheels instead of three. The disadvantage of the three-wheel saws is that they bend the blade through such tight curves that the blades do not last as long as they do with a two-wheel saw.

The most important specifications to consider when buying a bandsaw for cutting turning blanks are the cutting depth and width. The width, or throat, is the distance between the blade and the body of the saw.

If your maximum required diameter is 450mm (18in) you can easily cut a blank of this size on a bandsaw allowing 225mm (9in) between blade and body.

Bandsaw blades are mainly enclosed by the body of the saw, but where the cutting takes place they naturally have to be exposed. The amount of exposure is adjustable by means of a guide bar, which should be set at a height slightly above the surface of the wood to prevent fingers from straying onto the blade. The maximum depth of cut is determined by the maximum distance between the bottom of the guide bar and the saw table. You need to decide what sizes of blanks you are likely to want to cut and then allow an extra 50mm (2in), partly to cater for that extra thickness of cut you may need sometime, but also to ensure that the machine is strong enough to cut your usual dimensions on a regular basis.

I thought I'd never need to cut blanks thicker than 150mm (6in), so bought a saw with 200mm (8in) maximum depth. I've often wished I had gone for a 250mm (10in) depth, because this is sometimes needed when cutting up pieces of tree.

The motor strength required will depend on the maximum depth specification. Good-quality saws will have the commensurate size, which seems to be 0.75hp for 150mm (6in) up to 200mm (8in) upwards, and 1.5 hp for 200mm up to 250mm (10in).

Guide supports

The blades are supported above and below the table by guide supports, which may be solid metal with slits in, or thrust rollers. I find the solid ones wear out and are expensive to replace.

The roller types offer less resistance and may be offered as an alternative to solid ones when you buy the saw. They will initially be more expensive but will be worth it.

The solid types have to be adjusted so that the teeth are not enclosed in them, which wears away the kerf.

Many tables can be tilted, but although I rarely use this facility, I imagine it could be useful for some woodworkers.

One very useful accessory is a rip fence, used for cutting set widths such as spindle blanks. The wood must be pressed against the fence to ensure an even cut, and if the blade is blunt this is difficult, if not impossible.

Watch your fingers when using the rip fence, as the narrow widths mean that if the wood is pushed by hand your fingers will get very near the blade.

Bandsaw with door open showing three wheels and guards off.

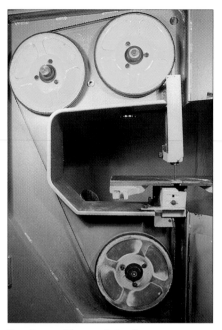

Bandsaw with guards in place.

You can also find that, because you are usually cutting with the grain using the rip fence, you must be aware that the wood can unexpectedly split along the grain and the wood suddenly shoot through. If you are pushing with your hand at the end of the wood, in line with the blade, it will result in a nasty accident.

Continuous blade

The blade is continuous, being welded. The quality of this weld is an important factor in the longevity of the blade. Because of the narrow width of the blade and the thinness of the steel the surface area available to make the joint is obviously small, so specialised equipment is needed to do it.

Blades for wood are usually made of carbon steel and are cut to length according to the specifications of the bandsaw. The two ends are welded together by passing a high current through them. This makes for a brittle joint which is not as flexible as the rest of the blade, so good engineers then temper the joint and file and polish it to make it run smoothly through the saw guides.

If you buy a blade which soon comes apart at the weld, you are entitled to expect the supplier to replace it. If it happens a second time, change your supplier.

To order blades you need to know not only the length but also the width. Most saws will take a range of sizes because this dimension affects the diameter of the circle you can cut. If you multiply the width by 10 this gives the approximate minimum diameter.

I never need to cut smaller than 100mm (4 in) diameter, so can do all my work with 13mm (½in) blades. This enables me to order 10 at a time, earning a discount from my supplier.

I tend to cut blanks with a diameter of less than 150mm (6in) by cutting the wood into squares and then cutting off the corners rather than doing it in one continuous cut to prevent the blade getting jammed in the tight curve. If you need to do a lot of straight cuts, the blade should be as wide as possible.

The other specification you need to know when ordering blades is the tooth format. This depends on the type of work you will do.

Regular formats are used for thin section materials such as plywood, plastics or non-ferrous metals and these can be obtained in 10,12 and 24 teeth per inch.

Skip formats

I use skip formats all the time, because it's useful for cutting thick and wet timber where a regular format would clog. I use three-tooth skip, which has the longest gap between the teeth but, you can also obtain four or six skip.

Bandsaw blades can be sharpened by hand, but whenever you do this you reduce the kerf (the amount by which the teeth stick out to each side of the blade). And it's such a laborious, time-consuming task that for the professional it's not worth it.

Blades are best thought of as disposable, but they should be changed as soon as they get blunt, because then you have to push the wood harder, causing the motor to overheat and increasing the danger of hands slipping on the wood and onto the blade.

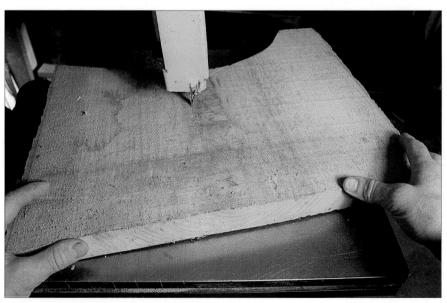

Cutting a platter blank marked out with dividers, hands out, away from the blade.

Cutting a spindle blank, using the fence and push sticks.

Advice for users

When cutting wet wood, sap can build up on the blade behind the teeth, impairing its passage through the guides. If you spray WD40 or duck oil on the blade while it's running, this will reduce the build up. When cutting thick planks, use a sharp blade and feed very slowly, or the blade will bend in the cut and the sides of the blank will be bellied.

If you press too hard the blade may jam in the cut and the bandsaw grind to a halt. There should be an overload switch to stop the motor, but I always hit the off button as soon as this happens, to reduce any possibility of the motor windings burning out.

When it happens, you have a problem of getting the blade out of the blank. The best way I've found of doing this is to insert a wedge into the beginning of the cut and open it up, so you can back the blade out. This is difficult if you are over half way around a blank, so I always cut large blanks in stages so the blade is never far from the beginning of the cut.

When I started using the bandsaw it was my only power saw, and I had to lift large lumps of wood onto the table. This resulted in a lot of jammed blades and did not do my back any good. I now cut the planks nearer to size with a chainsaw.

When cutting wet woods, particularly those containing tannin, such as oak, it's a good idea to spray the surface of steel parts with WD40 after you've finished, to prevent corrosion.

Bandsaws are potentially dangerous. The blade is enclosed and the section you are cutting with is just a blur, so it's easy to become blasé.

My worst injury was sustained while using a bandsaw, so now, every time I use it, I recall finding a small piece of finger bone on the saw table when I returned to the workshop after my trip to hospital and I am suitably cautious.

I always use a dust extractor fitted to the saw, because the dust produced is so fine it irritates the nose and clogs the inside of the saw.

I also wear a Racal Airstream helmet to filter out any escaping dust and save my eyes from flying offcuts. I put on ear defenders, because the high-pitched whine made by the blade can damage hearing.

Out of control

If you try to cut wood with an overhang, the force of the saw blade will try to push it down and will snatch it out of your control.

If you hold onto the wood your fingers can end up on the blade, and if you let go the wood can end up anywhere, certainly kinking the blade. Cutting across a cylinder is cutting an overhang so you must make a vee-shaped cradle to support it. Follow these safety rules:

- Keep fingers away from blade until it has stopped.
- Wear face guard and ear defenders.
- Use a dust extractor.
- Ensure the table is well lit.
- Keep the surrounding area clear.
- Do not try to cut an overhang.
- If cutting through a cylinder support it in a cradle.
- Lower blade guard to just above the surface of the wood.
- Do not push with your hand in line with the cut.
- Never use a blunt blade.
- Use a push stick for ripping. ∎

On the water front – seasoning

Problems associated with seasoning timber

The main problem with timber is that it has an annoying habit of changing shape if it is turned unseasoned. This is because the tree did not make the wood with turning in mind but to transport water and minerals up to the leaves.

As soon as this process is stopped by a chainsaw the wood starts to dry and because water is such a large percentage of the constituents of wood the volume goes down.

The growing tree has its lowest water content when the leaves have fallen, so if you have a choice it's best to fell a tree in winter, so that the seasoning process will be speeded up.

Humidity

The amount of water the timber loses depends on the water in the atmosphere (relative humidity), and once the water content is in equilibrium with the air, the timber won't change shape.

Sadly, the relative humidity of the air is not constant, except in houses with air conditioning, so if the timber is in equilibrium at one moment it will not always be so.

Just as timber can dry and shrink it can also absorb water and increase in volume, but because the volume changes are fairly small this is not usually much of a problem.

In temperate climes relative humidity changes are small, but in some parts of the world it can change from 0% to 100% in hours. All I can offer to turners in these conditions is my sympathy – you already know

Photo 1 **Log left in open to develop end shakes**.

not to buy too much wood before you need it.

If a turned object is made from wood with a high moisture content and it dries quickly it may well be altered out of all recognition by cracking or warping, so before you turn it you need to know how wet it is and what effect this will have on the resultant piece.

If it's just a little too damp it may only warp, and this is not necessarily a problem in the case of a bowl with a small base because it may only become slightly elliptical.

But it could a problem for a platter with a large base, which would then wobble, and it would be a serious disadvantage in a box with a tight-fitting

lid which would then either stick or be too loose.

The surface in contact with the air dries first and shrinks. If the process is rapid due to very hot, dry conditions, tensions will build and cracking occur, as the shrinking part is in contact with wood that has not had time to dry (because it is not in contact with the air).

In other words, if you try to dry a thick piece of wood too quickly it will crack. If wood is allowed to dry gently the water will be able to migrate from the inside to the outside without stresses building up.

It's easier to do this if the wood is in thin section, such as a 25mm (1in) plank and if it is not exposed to a howling gale and full sun.

Photo 2 **More examples of end shakes**.

face area so that the outside does not dry too much more quickly than the inside and it also releases the tension of the complete circle of annular rings. By doing this you effectively impose two radial shakes exactly where you want them.

The most efficient way of doing this in terms of non-renewable sources of energy is to use wedges and a large club hammer, but this does not work on some trees, such as elm, and if the grain is twisted you can waste a lot of material because of the unevenness of the surfaces produced.

Leaving bark on

Leaving the bark on the tree reduces the speed of transpiration from the natural surface, but if the bark drops off you may have to take similar measures to slow down drying from this surface.

If the tree is big enough, it's worth planking and stacking it. I like to have trees planked in 30mm (1¹/₄ in) boards for platters and breadboards.

They are delivered at once to my workshop, where I stand the planks on end in the open air for about a week, during which time a great deal of water drains from the end. I then stack them horizontally in my wood shed (*photo 3*).

Photo 4 shows a traditional stack done by putting the tree back together on large bearers, say 100mm

It's also a bad idea for wood to be rained on, because the alternate wetting and drying causes tensions, quite apart from the tendency for fungal discolouration.

A good source of turning timber is garden trees that are too small to interest sawmills. The best of these, in addition to commercial species, are the fruitwoods, laburnum, box, sumac, laurel and some eucalypts, but it's worth trying any exotic.

The only problem is how do you avoid end grain radial shakes as in photo 1. In this length of tree they may not extend all the way along, but if it had been cut into short lengths, as tree surgeons tend to do for firewood, the shakes would certainly have extended the full length. So the first thing to do is not to cut your tree into short lengths.

Short lengths

Photo 2 shows a fine selection of short lengths put to one side in a timber yard awaiting conversion. All display radial shakes induced by exposure to the sun and the shortest pieces are already useless.

The shakes are caused by the outside drying quicker than the inside, so the next thing to do is to slow this down by keeping the tree in the shade and then reducing the speed of evaporation even further by sealing the end grain.

I use a by-product of oil refining called emulsified paraffin wax, sold by Mobil as Mobilcer C in 22.5 Kg drums, but available from Craft Supplies in smaller quantities.

You can use candlewax, but this has to be melted and is therefore so potentially hazardous that I don't recommend it. PVA glue is effective but more expensive, and I have also successfully used old spirit-based paint. Putting a plastic bag over the ends would also work, but you would have to be careful about fungi growing in the air space.

Splitting the tree reduces the tendency to shake by increasing the sur-

Photo 3 **The author's drying shed**.

square (4 x 4in) with 17mm ($^{11}/_{16}$in) square slats (the old word is dunnage) between each plank.

These should be as wide as the plank and spaced at 60cm (2ft) intervals along it. They should also be above one another so that the weight of the planks presses down in a vertical line and reduces the tendency of the planks to warp.

Sometimes people nail wooden slats to the end of planks to prevent splitting, but this never seems effective if the large cracks I've seen beneath them are anything to go by.

I seal the end of planks with Mobilcer C and this usually saves much wastage. When I've applied this to the freshly-sawn end of a 100mm (4in) thick plank. I usually find I can use it right up to its end without coming across any shakes.

It's not a good idea to leave the stack in the open as in the photo, for rain tends to get between the planks and discolour them. The stack shown is ash and had been left in the open for a couple of years, by which time the outsides of most planks had gone grey as much as 150mm (6in) into the centre.

Buyer beware

It's always a case of let the buyer beware when buying timber, as some saw mill operators have terrible memories when asked how long a particular pile of timber has been sawn.

The stack in photo 4 has obviously been sawn for at least a year because it is so weathered, but the timber in photo 5 looks fresh. Wood is always at its most highly coloured when freshly sawn, and then quite quickly loses its bright colours.

When it is so grey that you cannot see the grain it may well have been sawn long enough to be seasoned, but it's wise to plane a sample to see whether it is the colour you want and to check for discoloration.

The rule of thumb for seasoning is that it takes a year to dry every 25mm (1in) of thickness. But that just means it will have achieved equilibrium and in wet parts of the British Isles, such as Devon, that is a maximum of 18%

Photo 4 **Timber well stacked but open to the elements.**

water content, and you need it to be down to at least 12% to be stable in a centrally-heated house. Eighteen per cent simply means it will not be prone to fungal attack.

I use a moisture meter to check the water content of my wood. This works by pushing two probes into the wood and measuring the electrical resistance.

As the outside is the driest part, you need to get the probes into the very centre. I do this by using it on offcuts during the blank cutting process or by carving away a chunk from the surface and putting the probes in there.

The Pin-Free moisture meters avoid this problem, and I've heard good reports about the effectiveness of the Wagner range, but have yet to test them.

If you don't have a moisture meter, the most accurate way of measuring water content is to cut a sample at least 200mm (8in) from the end of a board and immediately weigh it.

If there will be some delay, it should be sealed in a plastic bag because it must not be allowed to dry out or re-absorb moisture. The sample should be 25mm (1in) long and should be a full cross section. The weight should be written on the sample.

The sample should be dried by putting it in an oven heated to 214-

221° F (101-105° C) and left there until the weight stabilises. This will take from 12 to 48 hours. The water content can then be calculated using the following formula:

% water content = Weight when cut − dry weight x 100
Dry weight

If, for example, the sample weighs 8oz (226.8g) when cut and 7oz (198.4g) when dry, the water content is one-seventh of the dry weight, ie 14.3%.

When you buy a pre-cut blank with a label declaring it is part air dried, this might only mean that it was planked the day before it was cut into a circle and it may be very wet indeed.

Without a moisture meter the only way of finding out how wet it is will be to rough it out. I leave the wall thickness greater than usual (10% of the diameter works for ash) and weigh the bowl, writing on its base the weight and the date weighed.

If you leave it in a dry, cool atmosphere for a week and re-weigh it, you can see if it has lost weight. If it has, this means it is drying and should be left until it is stable in the atmosphere where it will be used.

I only work from solid blank to finished bowl where I am sure it is dry and has straight grain. If it is dry

Photo 5 **Stack of fresh planks.**

but the grain is curly, you can still get warpage because of the tensions released during hollowing.

I turn all my ash and burr oak bowls from unseasoned timber, because thick planks of seasoned wood are hard to find in the quantities I use.

Expensive

I've also found that thick seasoned planks tend to be more expensive per cube and more wasteful because they have cracks.

Drying large quantities of wood is difficult to do properly for a commercial concern partly because of the number of sheds needed to keep them under cover. But the main problem is that the air drying process is so difficult to control because of the widely fluctuating temperatures and humidity that occur even in Britain's climate.

Kiln drying timber is more controllable but needs a lot of specialised knowledge and equipment. What you can achieve varies with the species, but to dry planks more than 75mm (3in) thick, 50mm (2in) in the case of

oak, is not economic, because it is hard to guarantee that the inside has not stayed wet after the outside has dried.

When I have roughed out bowls from wet wood I leave them for a week or two in a cool part of my workshop to gradually start to dry, and then seal the end grain inside and out with Mobilcer C.

This is important because the two sides of the bowl where the end grain is exposed will dry much quicker than the other sides, and this can cause cracking or excessive distortion.

The slower the drying process and the drier the wood when turned the less it will warp and the fewer samples will be lost because of cracking.

If I need to produce ash salad bowls in a hurry I rough them out, seal the end grain and put them in a sealed cupboard with a domestic de-humidifier. Depending on how wet they were to start with they can be ready to finish within a month.

If I need to dry platter blanks from partially-air-dried timber, I cut them bigger than the required size and they also dry very nicely in the cupboard.

If you don't work in the quantities as I do, try using an airing cupboard, but put each bowl in a plastic bag so that drying does not take place too quickly. If the bag is turned inside out every day or so then the condensation can evaporate. ∎

Suppliers

Timber

Tiverton Sawmills, Blundells Road, Tiverton, Devon. Tel: 01884 253102.

Yandle & Sons Ltd, Hurst Works, Martock, Somerset. Tel: 01935 822207.

Craft Supplies, The Mill, Miller's Dale, Buxton, Derbyshire. Tel 01298 871636.

End grain sealer

Mobil Oil Company, Mobil House, 400-500 Witan Gate House, Central Milton Keynes Tel 01908 853344 Price £42 per 22.5 Kg drum plus small order charge of £17.50 plus VAT

Craft Supplies Price £13.45 per 5 litre inc VAT

Moisture meters

Wagner electronics, WMS Consulting Ltd, PO Box 312, Folkestone, Kent CT20 2GB. Tel: 01303 850822.

Protimeter plc, Meter House, Fieldhouse Lane, Marlow, Bucks SL7 1LX. Tel 01628 472722.

On the waterfront
Part Two

Re-turning a dry, burr oak bowl

In last month's article about seasoning, I mentioned that I rough out bowls from wet timber because of the problem of getting enough dry timber in 100mm (4in) thick planks, the size I need for salad bowls.

There are other advantages in this way of working. I can, for example, buy a whole tree from the sawmill and have it planked to my specifications. This is cheaper than buying it already seasoned and in small quantities.

Not everyone, I know, can handle a hundred cubic feet of unseasoned wood, but some of my techniques are relevant to less busy turners, who may have just a couple of wet blanks of ornamental cherry tree to deal with.

If you can rough out the wet wood as soon as you get it you will lose less of it because of degradation while seasoning, ie shakes and rotting, and

Inside the drying cupboard.

it will dry out quicker than it does in the plank. It helps if you have a wood-burning stove to use the offcuts when they have dried and to dispose of shavings. I give some shavings to a local horse owner for bedding, and use lots on the garden, where they serve as an excellent mulch, retaining water, depressing weeds and raising the organic content of the soil. Hamsters and gerbils like shavings as bedding, but there are not enough of them locally to make serious inroads into my by-products.

Main drawback

The only serious disadvantage of using this method is that the offcuts have to season before they can be used to make into small items and they tend to crack because of their size.

I keep 100 x 100mm (4 x 4in) section lengths because I use them for sugar bowls, but they have to be stored carefully with their ends sealed while they dry.

Once the roughed out bowls have dried, perhaps in an insulated cupboard or kiln with a de-humidifier, they can be re-turned as required.

When a kiln-full has seasoned, I put them in the workshop, which then has to be kept dry with a de-humidifier or the blanks would re-absorb moisture.

Re-turning dried-out bowls uses processes like those for re-mounting bowls to clean-up their bottoms, with the added difficulty that they will not be round when they have to be re-mounted.

When I started making large numbers of salad bowls, it was quite acceptable to turn them on a faceplate and fill with plastic wood the holes left by the screws. The process was quicker then.

I would rough out the bowls by screwing the bottom of the blank to a faceplate with two screws aligned along the grain so that the distance between them would diminish little after drying (wood shrinks more across the grain than with it).

I'd rough turn the outside and inside on this one fixing and, after drying, would usually be able to remount them using the same screw holes. I then finished off the inside and outside and cleaned-up the bottom on a sanding disc.

There is nothing wrong with this method for ordinary items – only fashion makes it no longer allowable. Why it should be unacceptable to have the evidence of mounting on the base of a bowl is hard to justify, and the honesty of visible screw holes has a naiveté I find appealing.

To me, they are much more aesthetically pleasing than the hard-edged recess needed by most chucks, as they don't interfere with the smoothness of the bottom.

Single-screw chuck

Having said that, I now use expanding dovetail jaws on my Axminster four-jaw chuck for all my roughing out, because it's quicker to mount the bowls initially on a single-screw chuck.

The recess on the bottom is easy to centre and takes up less depth in the base, which means if you hollow too deep you don't meet the screws. It's also quicker and easier to re-mount roughed out bowls on a recess than screws, and they sell better with the recess turned away than with screw holes. I also hate other turners looking at the bottom of my bowls and tutting.

Roughed out and dry burr oak bowl.

For most woods it's enough to seal the end grain to slow the drying of that part, for a more even speed of drying. But with burr oak I find it necessary to seal the whole surface, the grain being so wild that end grain can crop up anywhere. By the way, if I try to speed the drying of burr oak by putting it in the kiln too early, it usually cracks.

If the burr is consistent the bowl will distort fairly evenly and re-mounting is easy, but if there are patches of plain wood as well as burr, distortion can be so extreme that it's even impossible to re-turn.

If you buy your wood reasonably cheaply and turn a large quantity at great speed, this is not a major financial loss, but if this is not the case, the wasted effort can demoralise.

A good idea

If a bowl dries evenly and the dovetail jaws fit in the recess in the base, it's possible to re-turn the bowl just by re-mounting it on the same jaws it was originally turned on. But it's usually a good idea to mount the bowl by supporting it from the top and re-turning the recess, because even if the distortion seems small you get a better grip from a perfectly circular recess.

Rarely is everything as it seems.

Fitting the bowl on O'Donnell jaws.

Sometimes a bowl seems to have distorted little, but you find the top has shifted to the side relative to the bottom and to get the biggest bowl you have to re-mount from the top.

One way of re-mounting the bowl is to support it from the inside using O'Donnell jaws in a recess drilled by a saw-tooth bit on a pillar drill.

This makes a parallel-sided recess which is not gripped as securely as an overhung recess, but it has the advantage that the bowl can adjusted on its axis to maximise the available size.

You may need to use a shortened off ratchet spanner to expand the jaws as in the photo above, as the sides of the bowl may impede access to the chuck. Because of the relatively weak support of this method you have to take very light cuts when correcting the base recess.

There are many ways of holding the bowl from the top, but the method I prefer because of its flexibility is the wood jaw plates of the Axminster four-jaw.

I use the 125mm (5in) chuck (no longer available), which gives a wider range of sizes for each set of jaws than the 100mm (4in) chuck. You can make jaws for the 4in which give a fair range of sizes, but it's not as good as the three different sets for the range of diameters – 20mm(8in) to 450mm(18in) – that I have.

Making wood jaws

There are many different ways of making the wood jaws, largely depending on the bowl design, but provided your design has sides roughly parallel at the top, my design will work. Full instructions are in my book, *Turning Bowls: Step by Step*, published by BT Batsford.

It's just as easy to make jaw plates that expand into the bowl by making the steps in reverse if your bowl design lends itself to this (e.g. an overhang).

It is important to make the top of the bowl as flat and round as possible before you mount the bowl. If the top isn't flat, you should first flatten the bottom. This will be smaller than the top so easier to do. Once you've planed it flat with a hand plane, power plane, sanding disc or Arbotech, you'll see how much work you need do to make the top parallel to it.

I usually rotate the bowl in one

Drilling a recess inside the bowl.

Making the outside concentric.

Side view of bowl in wooden jaws.

hand while planing the top, so that I remove the high points, and assess the levelness by eye – there is no need to be completely accurate.

If the bowl has warped evenly when seen from the top, so that it is elliptical, you can probably grip it well enough to support it while you make the recess true, because an ellipse will give you four points of contact in four-jaws.

But if the bowl is very elliptical or wildly distorted, you may have to make it round by scribing a circle on the top with callipers. I put a block of wood inside so that the centre point of the callipers is level with the top, otherwise they won't work.

Cut around marks

I then bandsaw round the marks. Where there's an overhang I press hard down on the opposite side of the bowl and feed the cut very slowly.

It's safer to cut with the top of the bowl on the saw table and guessing where the marks are, erring on the conservative side and often turning the bowl over to check where they are.

The bowl should now fit snugly in the jaws, but I always run the lathe very slow to true-up the base, only increasing the speed when I'm sure the support is secure. I work towards the centre with a 9mm (⅜ in) or 6mm (¼ in) bowl gouge, taking very light cuts and aiming the gouge at the outermost blurred surface.

This will feel dodgy at first because the tool wants to follow the uneven surface, but you need to know the angle at which you have to hold the gouge and press it firmly on the tool rest at that angle while you pass the tool along the rest.

As with most gouge cuts, the flute should be pointing in the direction of cut and the cutting should be done with the bottom half of the nose. If the bevel is almost rubbing, it should not dig in.

You do this until the base is flat. Sometimes, at this stage, the old recess has disappeared. I simply mark

out a new one and carry on as usual, but if a recess is left I true the bottom with the small gouge and then make the sides the correct dovetail for the chuck with my square-ended scraper ground at the correct angle.

The Axminster four-jaw chuck has such a wide range of movement and I have such a good selection of jaws to choose from that I do not have to worry about the size of the recess.

If your chuck is less forgiving, you will have to leave enough wood in the base of your roughed out bowls to make a new recess of the correct size.

Front view of trued-up bowl in wood jaws.

Starting to true-up the inside.

The outside cut nearing the rim.

I always ensure I can re-mount a piece in case it works free, but having established the recess often true up the outside of the bowl, taking very light cuts again. When I reverse the bowl using the recess it's easier to see that it is concentric if the sides are true.

It's safer not to go too near the top of the bowl, in case the gouge slips onto the chuck jaws.

The re-mounted bowl can be re-turned using gouges, in much the same way as turning a bowl from the solid. I make the rim flat first, then stop and see if there are any cracks in the wood. I then take off the high points inside and do the same to the outside so that I can see exactly how much wood is left to play with. This also makes the bowl concentric so that it rotates evenly on the lathe without excessive vibration.

Although I usually true up the outside of the bowl near the base when it is mounted by the top, it's usually necessary to turn all the way round the sides when the bowl is mounted on the recess, to give the sides the curve I want.

This is easy enough so long as the lathe lets the tool rest go around the side to support the gouge, and provided the bowl's base is bigger than the diameter of the body of the chuck.

If not, you need to turn the bottom section of the side when removing the recess on the base, in which case it's difficult to blend into the already-finished section. Or, you can use O'Donnell jaws, which give such a projection from the chuck that you can get access all the way to the base. Bob Chapman also makes jaws which fit several makes of chuck for this purpose.

The bowl can now be finished as if it was being made from the solid. ■

Making the outside concentric near the base.

Suppliers

Chuck, jaws, pillar drill and saw tooth bit from:
Axminster Power Tool Centre, Chard Street, Axminster, Devon EX13 5DZ. Tel (orders only): 0800 371822. Fax: 01297 35242.

Alternative jaws from:
BCWA, 93 Parkway, Coxheath, Maidstone, Kent ME17 4EX. Tel: 01622 747325.

Workshop layouts

Increasing your efficiency with a well-planned workshop

I love visiting workshops, seeing how other people organise their tools and imagining what I could make from their offcuts.

Several furniture-making friends of mine have purpose-built mini factories with smooth floors, well-placed windows, well-spaced machinery, electricity delivered in proper conduits. They have specially-made cupboards for tools, racks for timber and dust extractors to keep things tidy and the atmosphere pure.

I've never seen a woodturner's workshop like that. Most of us seem to use sheds that were designed for something else. They are full of cupboards rescued from places to which dead furniture has been consigned and have shelves made of floorboards so old that even the wood-worm turn their noses up at them.

They are stacked with roughed-out bowls, offcuts that will come in useful, sometime, and discarded wonder tools that never worked as well for us as they did for the magzine reviewer or demonstrator at the show.

I like to think that keeping all manner of objects, "in case they come in useful", is an admirable trait of a practical person. But it's a position not above criticism from some quarters.

Space problems

Space problems are involved. How long do you keep the jig that took a day to make to save you five minutes work for a job you will never do again? A good time is when you are half-way through making an exact replica before you realise there is something very familiar about what you are doing.

And is there really any point in keeping the stubs of worn out gouges? Just because they are High-Speed Steel are they likely ever to be useful for anything?

My present workshop is heaven compared to where I started – in a corner on the first floor of a watermill at a Devon craft centre.

I taught myself to turn on a lathe made from a kit mounted on a rickety bench concealing my book of instructions.

My dust extractor was an open outside door and window, my saw a circular blade mounted on the lathe spindle – not a system I'd recommend.

When I left the craft centre, weary of being in the public gaze, I needed a house with workshop attached. The only way my partner and I could afford this was to buy an old shippen (cowhouse) lately used as a workshop. It was situated in a builder's yard, where there was a fine array of sheds.

We converted the shippen into a house and I took over the sheds to use as workshop, timber store and showroom.

The biggest shed was 13.7m (45ft) long by 4.6m (15ft) wide – railway sleeper uprights supporting a tiled roof, clad with corrugated iron and asbestos sheets. It had a concrete floor, but no damp-proof course. I had the good fortune to win a major award from South West Arts to buy my own lathe, and got a loan from the Crafts Council to improve one end of the shed so that I had an area large enough to install my machinery. It was small and well-insulated enough to heat efficiently.

The area is 4.6m (15ft) by 4.6m, big enough for two Graduate lathes, one short bed and one long, plus a bandsaw, dust extractor, benches and cupboards.

The rest of the workshop tends to be damp, as I live in a damp part of a damp county. So tools rust and wood does not remain totally dry.

That part of the workshop is, however, very useful for slowly drying timber in plank, tree or roughed-out-bowl form. And it's the home of my insulated cupboard which contains a de-humidifier for bowl drying.

There is also a heap of assorted cardboard boxes for sending products to shops – and sometimes room for the car.

Timber store

Outside the workshop is my timber store, an area covered with corrugated iron but open at the side to let air circulate while keeping off the rain. There is usually room for me to chainsaw planks into blanks under shelter. Although it is open to the air, I prefer to use an electric chainsaw there, as fumes from a petrol saw can linger when there is no wind.

It's also better to use an electric saw for intermittent sawing, because a petrol saw works better when used continuously. I always use a circuit breaker on the socket when doing this, as you can accidentally cut through the lead.

An essential piece of kit for me is the wheelbarrow in which I carry lumps of wood to the workshop. When I've emptied it I park it on the other side of the saw and simply push the offcuts into it, before transporting them to the firewood shed.

I have a range of products I supply to certain customers, and a list on the

Workshop with blinds up.

bandsaw of the blank sizes they are made from. When I cut dry timber into circular blanks I convert, say 50mm (2in) thick planks into 255mm (10in), 230mm (9in), 200mm (8in), 125mm (5in), or 100mm (4in) diameters. I then cut the offcuts into 41mm (1⅝ins) x 41mm x various lengths for products such as scoops and honey dippers.

I'm careful to use only straight-grained offcuts for this and also reject timber in any other way inferior, such as discoloured or soft, because I know that the latter are not saleable and if the grain is twisted it takes longer to turn between centres.

Tea chests

Near the bandsaw I keep a stack of tea chests on their sides with hard-board over the bottom half of the open ends, in which to store offcuts according to sizes and species.

Some people store and saw their timber in places other than where they turn. But I find that if I have to mount an out-of-shape blank and the bandsaw is in a different room, it's tempting not to bother with the safer and quicker option of cutting it circular on the saw. It would also mean insulating another area.

My workshop has evolved to help my way of working. A typical process is to spend a day roughing bowls. I

cut 20 to 30 blanks from 100mm (4in) thick ash, varying from 150mm (6in) diameter to 450mm (18in).

I drill holes for a single-screw chuck in them, up to 350mm (14in) diameter, using an ATPC floor-standing drill press near the bench. Larger bowls are mounted on a faceplate, using a cordless drill for the holes and screws.

Pull down blinds

I pull down blinds behind me so shavings do not cover the shelves, and block up the benchgrinder. I don't have to worry about the Tormek grinder, which has a cover which prevents the trough filling with shavings.

I turn the outsides of the blanks on the inboard side of the lathe and form recesses for the APTC four-jaw chuck. The recess sizes which work for my designs and skills are 63mm (2½in) for sizes over 300mm (12in) and 38mm (1½in) for the rest, but beginners would be safer with larger sizes for stability. I then hog out the insides, dating each one as I finish it.

The sharpening systems are mounted just behind me, so that I don't have far to go when the tool needs sharpening. And they are at heights which enable them to be used without bending.

It's important to have sharpening systems to hand, because it is much

When the blinds are down, shavings don't cover shelves and block the benchgrinder.

without a hiccup. Indeed, it so improved my turning efficiency that I would not want to be without it.

I have a floor of flooring grade chipboard on top of expanded polystyrene, which improves the comfort of my feet. I once thought lathe vibrations were absorbed by this and that I did not need to bolt-down the lathe.

In fact I read that if one did so, the vibrations of turning would come back up through the lathe and do it harm. But I became so impressed by the stability of other turners' bolted-down lathes that I decided to do the same.

Chasing the lathe

I'd tired of chasing the lathe around the floor, although this at least enabled me to sample all possible positions. I decided the best place was near a window and far enough from the wall to swing the biggest object the lathe would ever take.

Sadly, the floor was so shoddily made – of 38mm (1½ins) concrete on a layer of rubble – that I had to dig a hole and fill it with concrete to hold the bolts firmly.

Since doing this, the benefits of having a steady lathe have been obvious. At certain speeds some blanks cause vibrations, but with variable speed you can increase or

safer and more efficient to use a sharp tool than a blunt one.

You should not start turning without some sharpening device, even if it's only the cheapest Asiatic version, and there are sharpening jigs to suit all pockets and machines. So there's no excuse not to keep your tools sharp.

After a day spent roughing-out bowls, the wheelbarrow comes into play again, first to transport the piles of shavings onto the garden

and then to shift the many bowls into the outer part of the workshop.

There they are stacked on their sides for a week until I treat the end grain with end-grain sealer. If I need them in a hurry they may be dried quickly in the kiln, or if not I store them on racks just under the roof.

The lathe I use for all my bowl work is a short bed Graduate, refurbished and fitted with Variturn and a 1½ hp motor by L.R.E Machinery in 1992. Since then it has served me

Grinding equipment.

Workshop showing position of bandsaw.

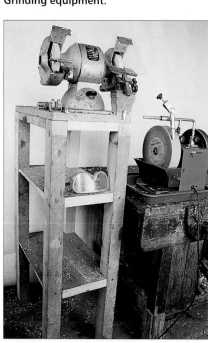

decrease this by a fraction and solve the problem.

I keep gouges, chisels and chucks in the tool box next to the lathe, where they are ready to hand. The tools in use for a particular job are kept on top of the box, which is at such a height that I do not have to bend to pick them up.

The box is on castors so that it can be moved as close as possible to the lathe. In the photo opposite it's in bowl turning position, but for short spindles it is put at the end of the tailstock.

Lighting

Lighting is vital for turning. I have an old dentist's lamp fitted to the wall, which can be moved over the work. And I have attached an angle-poise lamp to this, which points into the work.

Another angle-poise directed light onto the back of a bowl, but I've replaced this with an APTC lamp. This gives more light and has a covered bulb for more safety and ease of cleaning.

Dust extraction in a turner's workshop is always a problem, rotating work throwing it out at all angles and sanding producing much fine dust.

The problem is not that dust makes you sneeze, but that the very finest avoids nasal hairs and mucous and ends up clogging the lungs. And some timbers produce dust which is toxic or carcinogenic, or causes allergies in some people.

I mainly use ash or oak, which

Lathe tool box and window.

so far as I know are not toxic or carcinogenic. I avoid using exotic timbers, which include some really bad characters, apart from environmental considerations.

I have a dust extractor with hood near the lathe, made from half a 22.5 kilo tin drum. It's not very close, because I don't want it to pick up shavings.

Bandsaw connected

My bandsaw is also connected to the extractor. I know the unit should be outside the workshop to direct the fine dust which gets through the filter out of the way, but I tried that and froze in the winter. I wear an Airstream helmet all the time instead and this also protects my face against flying objects.

I keep electrical tools out of the way, in cupboards, along with hand tools and jigs, or they get covered with shavings.

I buy five different grades of cloth-backed aluminium oxide abrasives in reels and keep them on a wall rail, ready to tear off as needed.

Part-used pieces are kept in marked margarine containers in a plastic storage box, with a lid to keep shavings out.

I keep just one piece of each grade of abrasive in each little box so I can easily remember which grade

comes next in the sequence. I rarely need to work out what grade a piece of abrasive is by feel or by looking at the back.

Obviously, all workshops are different, according to the work being done, the level of activity engaged in and the turner's character. Whether you think my workshop is an untidy mess or a good example of how to achieve maximum efficiency for minimum outlay and brilliant organisation is up to you.

I only know that it works, and hope some of the things I've described will be of use to someone else or at least suggest the answer to a layout problem. ▪

Suppliers

Axminster Power Tool Centre, Chard Street, Axminster, Devon, EX13 5DZ. Tel: 0800 371822. Fax: 01297 35242.

L.R.E Machinery and Equipment Co, Bramco House, Turton Street, Golborne, Warrington WA3 3AB. Tel: 01942 272323 Fax: 01942 728208.

A typical group of Summer School pupils, with their teacher, Dave Regester, in shorts.

The right course

The questions to ask before deciding on a turning course

Woodturning has changed a lot since I started in the early 1970s. There were only a few books, and tools and lathes were hard to come by. Above all, it seemed to be a craft to make a living at, not a hobby.

If you could make a consistent range of well designed and finished turned items it was fairly easy to sell them, because there were few competitors.

Now there are so many books it is difficult to choose between them. Lathes, tools and pre-cut blanks are available by mail-order and there are

woodturning clubs all over the country.

Dozens of turning courses are advertised, and there are even videos to show how the expert does it again and again, even backwards if you like.

Today, woodturning is more popular as a hobby than as a job and many of the hobbyists are producing work good enough to sell.

Because they do not have the overheads of a professional there is no obvious reason why they should charge a competitive price. As it becomes harder for professionals to

make a living from turnery, many of them teach and so it goes on.

If you have decided that you would like to turn, how do you start? Many get the bug because a friend has just taken it up and is turning chunks of wood into something useful that looks good to the untutored eye. They often spend time with their friend, who is glad to show them how 'tis done for no charge.

Nothing wrong with that you may say and if someone who teaches for a living disagrees it is obviously sour grapes. But is it? Ask yourself

90 *Woodturning – an individual approach*

Mr Green using the facilities at Parnham (face mask removed for identification purposes).

what you look for when choosing a teacher for driving a car, for instance.

That requires skill and there is an element of danger if you make a mistake. So you would not select someone who had just passed their test, because they would not have the experience to help you with all the problems you might meet.

With turning you do not have to pass a test before you can teach, so the prospective pupil must work harder to find a suitable teacher.

Experience does not guarantee teaching ability but it is certainly a plus factor. It does not help if someone who has been turning a long time can't communicate how they do it.

A good teacher must show or describe every step, which means he has to have analysed why his method works.

Join a club

If I were starting to turn, I'd first join a turning club, preferably one affiliated to the Association of Woodturners of Great Britain (AWGB), and would attend a few meetings watching demonstrators and getting to know other members.

I've suggested this to some novices, who say these clubs are for people who already turn. Not so! Every club needs members who are at the bottom of the learning curve, so that everyone else feels superior and seems very knowledgeable when asked the simplest of questions.

Unlike many other activities, there is no long-established national

standard for turning and teaching turning. In mid-April, last year, a woodturning NVQ was accredited by the City and Guilds, so there is at least some standard qualification that woodworking students can aspire to.

Getting this took much work by members of the Register of Professional Turners, backed by The Worshipful Company of Turners, after previous attempts by the AWGB, and it's an important step in establishing the craft. But it's not really relevant to the aspiring hobbyist who is not interested in getting a qualification but in learning how to turn.

Questions to ask

What the aspiring turner needs to know about a possible teacher is:
● Can he or she turn?
● Can he or she teach?
● Are the facilities good enough?
● Can I afford the course?

The only woodturning body that tries to check the ability of its members is the Register of Professional Turners. Each prospective member is checked by an existing member in the

same area, so it's not standardised on a national basis.

The truth is that there can be no completely objective standard to establish whether someone is a good turner, but if a person is on the Register they will at least have been scrutinised.

Teaching qualification

As to whether a person can teach, there is nothing that even aspires to being a system of accreditation. Anyway, we all know from our school days there are plenty of examples of teachers who are qualified but quite unable to perform. Those who have a teaching qualification in another discipline and now teach turning, obviously have a grounding in general teaching techniques, but personality compatibility is more difficult to establish.

Once you have got to know a few people you will have a good idea who to ask for personal recommendations about teachers.

You can also tell from a show or club demonstration if you get along with the demonstrator and if he makes the sort of things you want to make and is willing to tell you how. Look at videos and read books and articles, paying as much attention to the person behind them and what they doing, as to following what they are saying in a practical sense.

When I started I had no money and thought I could not afford a teacher, so I spent many months turning full time and struggling to work out how the tools worked. Things would go right one day but not another, and I had no idea why.

Determination

I had more determination than sense and would have saved money in the long run if I'd taken lessons. The trouble with having no money is that you cannot even go into debt. Thankfully, my partner helped me.

Once you've found a good teacher it's vital to discover what their facilities are. Will there be good quality lathes, efficient sharpening devices; will tools be provided if you do not have your own? You cannot learn to turn on bad lathes. No-one can work efficiently on poor machinery.

Course prices vary and so does the ability to pay, but once you've found a good teacher it will probably make sense to wait until you

can afford that particular course than spend less on an unknown and perhaps inferior one.

You must also find out if the price is all inclusive or whether you will have to pay extra for wood etc.

I don't recommend you to buy a lathe and start on your own as I did, unless you are as desperate as I was. Apart from not knowing what you are doing with the tools it may be that the lathe you have bought is no good and is contributing to your lack of progress. You will not know what a sharp tool looks like and you will not know the safety considerations.

Day courses

A day's course with a good teacher is enough to get you started and you should ask as many questions as you can to find out what tools, lathe and benchgrinder to buy. Two days is usually enough to introduce you to bowl and spindle turning, but the essential factor in learning is the practice you put in. Make simple things first to become familiar with tools and equipment.

Making shavings from turning and sparks from sharpening is more impor-

tant than finishing a bowl or saving tool steel when you are learning.

If you want a thorough grounding in turning, consider a week's residential course at one of the Summer Schools, such as Parnham College in Beaminster, Dorset, where I teach.

An advantage of spending a week at such a place is that you get plenty of time to practise what you are taught. Learning is reinforced by doing. What you find easy one day you can have forgotten by the morrow unless you repeat it.

You also get plenty of time to ask all those questions you meant to ask, but forgot, in two days cramming.

When taking a course, I start by telling students how the lathe works and name the parts, so that when I say tighten the tailstock they know what I am referring to. I also get everyone to change the speed.

I tell them safety rules such as avoiding the danger zone and what to check before starting the lathe. These include checking the speed and ensuring the toolrest does not contact the work.

Make a bowl

I then teach them how to make a bowl. I once would start by teaching spindle turning, as that clearly shows how the grain direction affects the way tools work. But I've since found that most pupils find this more difficult than bowls, so now start with bowl turning. All my students succeed in making one, so gaining the confidence needed to tackle spindles.

Some learn better if the process is described in words and others if it's demonstrated. So I first give an overview of a whole process in simple terms and then demonstrate the first step – deciding which will be the top of the bowl and fixing a faceplate to it.

When all pupils have the bowl on the lathe, I check that everything is safe before demonstrating how to level the bottom with the bowl gouge.

With large groups I often get each pupil in turn to do a particular cut in front of everyone and then, if it is done correctly, general praise is

Chris Wilson, of Kent, with his project.

Dr Mellish, from the USA, with his raindrop project.

given. If success is not immediate, everyone has a chance to say why.

In this way pupils get into the habit of analysing every feature of tool use, so that when they try it they can better understand that there is a reason why things work or do not.

In groups where everyone is fairly extrovert this method often encourages camaraderie, and pupils often help each other out when teacher is occupied with someone else. But I take care not to impose this system on shy people.

Early stages

The early stages of a course are particularly difficult for everyone involved. The teacher has to work specially hard to assess not only the relative abilities of the pupils but also how best to teach them.

Teaching is a two way process which is hard work for both teacher and pupil. But when it goes well, all parties will learn. The more I teach the more I learn about teaching and woodturning.

It's tempting to think that once you have a grounding in basic techniques and have practised them you would not benefit from more tuition. And if

you are totally happy with what you are doing, so be it. But I know that if I wanted to do more hollow-form turning I'd benefit greatly from a course with Melvyn Firmager, for example, because he has solved all the problems connected with that branch of the craft. It would take years to sort them out myself.

Likewise, if you wanted to learn about new ideas and develop a more creative approach, you might choose a course like the one I ran at Parnham in 1997, called *On and off the lathe*. In it, I expected pupils to use some techniques other than turning to add to their turned piece.

I taught three pupils for a week and, after a couple of days revision of skills, showed them slides and photos of the work of innovative turners and gave them a short dissertation by Richard Hooper.

It's not enough to simply say, "Be more creative", and leave it at that. If someone wants help to extend themselves they need directions.

Ideas, in your own time, can take weeks to gestate, but in a pressured situation you need a goal. I gave students the idea of expressing motion,

and it was fascinating to see how the expression of something through woodturning could stimulate some into a rare burst of creativity but turn off others.

We are used to turned objects expressing smoothness or roughness, heaviness or lightness. But to convey a more specific idea needs analysis of that idea and a search for existing objects which suggest it.

I'd thought of a few ideas of my own to suggest motion, such as waves, a boat, even just a wheeled object.

One student, Dr Mellish, decided to depict the moment when a drop of water has bounced off the surface of a pool. His project was very well finished and suggested an upward motion.

Chris Wilson's idea was to produce an asymmetrical object with textured and stained surfaces which conveyed the feeling of movement in an abstract way.

Stimulate

The thinking behind advanced courses such as this one is not necessarily to produce finished objects of great merit (though this one certainly did), but to stimulate students to explore different ideas and help them with the techniques needed to express these thoughts.

I got a very positive feedback from my students, and similar courses may follow.

It would be easier to choose courses if there was an objective guide to consult, but without one I hope my suggestions as to what to look for will help you decide what questions to ask.

In the mean time, if anyone has any experiences to share it would be helpful if they wrote in to the Editor about them. ∎

Parnham Summer School, Parnham House, Beaminster, Dorset DT8 3NA. Tel: 01308 862204. Fax 01308 863444.

1 A basic tool kit for a beginner's course. From the top: bowl turning tools – 19mm (¾in) round-nosed scraper, 12mm (½in) square-ended scraper, 9mm (⅜in) bowl gouge; spindle tools – 19mm (¾in) spindle roughing gouge, 9mm (⅜in) spindle gouge, beading and parting tool, and a 19mm (¾in) oval skew chisel.

The art of course turning

The facts to assess when selecting a turning course

L ast month I made the point that because there is no nationally agreed standard for turning courses you have to use your initiative when selecting one.

Personal recommendation is a good guide, failing which the onus is on you to find out something about the tutor, to see if he or she is likely to know his or her stuff and is the sort of person you can spend time with.

Before paying out good money for a turning course you should get a prospectus, so that you know what your tutor intends to teach. If you are a complete beginner, you will need a course aimed at those with no experience.

If you are not sure what branch of turning you want to do, go for a course teaching both spindle and bowl turning. But if you know you want to do one or the other, select a specialised course.

Courses can also be tailored for those who have some experience but know they need help in learning correct techniques. It's quite difficult for a tutor to iron out bad habits which have been practised for years.

I find that if I demonstrate better methods it's possible to convince most experienced students that it's worth spending time to learn them.

If there's no description of the workshop in the brochure it's up to the prospective student to find out if it is well equipped, with enough good-quality lathes for each person and that there are adequate sharpening facilities, i.e. one benchgrinder for every three students.

Some prospectuses promise that students will complete many items in a short time, and if that is what you want then go for it.

My approach is to concentrate on teaching skills and to impart high standards of workmanship, so that fewer pieces are made, but hopefully more technique is remembered. I tell students what tools I shall be teaching them to use and add that if they have their own tools I'm happy for them to use them.

I make sure I have a stock of the tools I recommend, so I can sell them to the students if they need them. Learning the names of the tools and what they are for is an important early lesson. (See photo 1).

Fairly soon, I like to show students examples of my work, so they can see I am reasonably competent at turning and that I want them to learn high standards of design and finish.

Instill confidence

I tell them I've been turning since 1974 and that I produce a wide range of utilitarian and one-off pieces, so they can feel confident I've found answers to many of the problems they are likely to face.

The most important thing to get students to understand is that I want them to learn and that if I fail to convey that knowledge then I am at fault.

They must be encouraged to ask for clarification if they do not understand or have forgotten something, and the teacher must be patient enough to repeat information and keep thinking of different ways of saying things.

Each student has a unique intellect, education, experiences and degree of manual dexterity, and the trigger that gets him or her to do an operation efficiently has to be discovered by the teacher.

Turning is basically a very simple

Suppliers

Klein Design Lathe: Klein Design Inc., 17910 SE 110th St., Renton WA 98059 - 5323 USA. Tel: 206-226-5937. Fax: 206-226-2756.
Crown Tools: Excelsior Works, Burnt Tree Lane, Hoyle Street, Sheffield S3 7EX UK. Tel: 0114-272-3366. Fax: 0114-272-5252.
Reconditioned and upgraded Graduate lathes available from: L.R.E. Machinery & Equipment Co, 'Bramco House', Turton Street, Golborne, Warrington, WA3 3AB UK. Tel: 01942-272323. Fax: 01942-518290.

---

activity, but every pass of the tool is complex if you analyse the physical movements involved.

You can stand at someone's shoulder and produce a bowl with them by telling them what to do. But to impart all the knowledge needed to repeat that operation unsupervised calls for the conveyance of a lot of background information and the teaching of peripheral skills such as timber selection, cutting and seasoning and, most importantly, tool sharpening.

As a teacher you must remember to impart all the things you take for granted, while as a student you must remember that information, preferably by taking notes.

I demonstrate, describe verbally and, when necessary, hold the tool at the same time as the student, but the final process comes down to their practising at the lathe.

At this stage learning by mistake is effective, but the teacher has to be aware that mishaps are possible and judge when it's prudent to step in. One tries to prevent accidents that are likely to lead to loss of blood.

Safety rules

It's vital to tell students that turning involves sharp tools and rotating lumps of wood that can cause injury, but that this risk can be minimised by the following:
● Wearing a face shield or goggles to protect the eyes when turning or sharpening tools.
● Wearing a face mask to reduce the inhalation of dust.
● Wearing a smock or overalls that can be left in the workshop to reduce transporting dust to other environments.
● Wearing stout shoes to save the feet from falling tools or pieces of wood.
● By not wearing jewellery or any loose clothing that may catch in the lathe or wood.
● Tying up long hair.

Safe practices
● Tightly secure the wood to the lathe.
● Rotate the wood by hand before you start the lathe to check it will not snag on the toolrest.

● Check that the lathe speed is appropriate to the size of the object to be turned.
● When starting the lathe, stand away from the 'line of fire' – the area where the wood is most likely to fly if it detaches itself, at right angles to the axis of the lathe in line with the wood.
● Put the tool on the toolrest before touching the rotating wood with it.
● For faceplate work, position the toolrest so the tool can pass across the centre of the work when used at the correct angle (gouges and chisels point up and scrapers point down).

Workshop safety
● Keep the floor clear and the workshop tidy.
● Isolate electrical machinery before attempting any repair.
● Dispose of oily rags safely, as they can spontaneously combust if left exposed to the air.
● Don't turn under the influence of drink or drugs or when you are feeling tired.

The lathe

The most important functions of the lathe are how to turn it on and off and how to change the speed. Although many modern lathes have variable speed, many old ones still in use rely on belt changing, and it's essential students can do this.

Variable speed lathes have many advantages, but it's not always easy to see what speed they are on before starting a project. You must check this, as a large bowl might fly off if the lathe was accidentally started at a high speed.

Both teacher and student have to use the same terms for each part of the machine to avoid instructions being misunderstood. So the vital parts of the lathe should be named by the teacher as well as their function.

The headstock is the business end where the power comes from. A spindle runs through it with a threaded end onto which a faceplate or chuck can be fitted. It will usually be hollow so that a driving centre can be inserted for turning spindles between centres over the bed

Spindle thread of Union Graduate lathe.

(inboard). See photo 2. If the spindle passes right through the headstock so that bowls can be turned on the other end (outboard) it may be hollow all the way through, in which case the driving centre will be held in place by the taper of its shaft matching the taper of the hollow (photo 3). This usually conforms to standard measurements which are classified as Morse tapers, usually 1,2 or 3.

Four-pronged centre.

In the Klein Design lathe the driving centre is screwed onto a shaft which passes through the spindle and is held in place by the nut in the wooden flywheel (photo 4).

Driving centre of Klein Design lathe.

The driving centre grips the end of a spindle blank by means of two or four chisel-shaped projections called dogs or forks, and it has a central point which locates into the centre of the end of the spindle blank.

The dogs must be kept sharp or they will not grip and the centre should also be kept in good condition. These are often damaged by high speed collision with the lathe bed or floor when being inexpertly ejected from the spindle.

The driving centre is held in place by friction and if the lathe has a hollow spindle they are ejected by means of thrusting a tommy bar through the hollow.

If you grip the centre with your

hand (avoiding the sharp bits) and use minimal force on the tommy bar, remedial action on blunt bits is less often required (photo 5).

If your grip is too slack, a file or benchgrinder will remedy the damage, as the metal used for the driving centre is fairly soft.

As you look at the spindle from the inboard side it rotates in an anti-clockwise direction, so the thread on it is like a normal screw. A faceplate or chuck will tighten as the spindle turns.

The thread should be kept clean so that the faceplate screws all the way to the register at the end. Likewise, the faceplate thread must be free of gunge.

If it does not, the faceplate will not be concentric and/or the faceplate may become stuck. Other causes of intransigent chucks are leaving them on the lathe after use so that they cool down and shrink tight, or having a heavy catch.

You remove the offending object by immobilising the spindle with tommy bar or spanner and jerking the faceplate in an anti-clockwise direction. Steady pressure is not as effective.

If the faceplate remains, you must increase the effective diameter by screwing an iron bar to two screw holes or strike the back of the plate with a cold chisel, remembering to smooth the resultant scar with a file so you don't catch yourself on the burr.

Gripping centre when ejecting.

KLEIN DESIGN INC.
17910 SE 110TH STREET
RENTON, WASHINGTON 98059
(206) 226-5937

Three or four-jaw chucks can grip an iron bar to be levered free and chucks needing 'C' spanners can be removed if you add an extension bar to the end of the handle.

The size of spindle and type of thread varies from lathe to lathe, so faceplates and chucks will often not fit different makes of lathe, although many chucks have replaceable backing plates to cater for this problem.

If the lathe has an outboard spindle for bowl turning and the direction of rotation is not reversible the thread on this side will be in the opposite direction to the inboard side, so the chuck or faceplate will not unscrew. This means faceplates and chucks cannot usually be used on both sides of the lathe unless they have a double thread. I had one of my chucks double threaded by Axminster Power Tool Centre, and this is an obvious boon.

The toolrest supports the tool and is adjustable up, down and around in a toolrest support which can also be moved on the bed (photo 6). It's important the student understands how this is done and that the surface of the rest is kept free of indentations which impede the passage of the tool. This is done by locking the toolrest in place and filing the top surface.

First project

The first project I give beginners is to turn a bowl so they can achieve an acceptable product at the end of their first day and gain confidence before tackling the relatively more complex subject of spindle turning. I try not to confuse matters by talking at length about the tailstock before it is strictly relevant.

Next month I'll deal with the bowl gouge, its sharpening and use. ■

Olive ash
salad bowl,
250mm (9 ¾ins)
x 100mm (4in).

A first turning
project for
beginners

Getting started

A shallow bowl makes an excellent first project for beginners, whether on a course or struggling in their own workshop, because few tools are needed and some sort of bowl is usually produced.

Even if your bowl takes an age to make and the finish and design is not first class, you'll find it exciting to hollow a lump of wood and reveal the beauty of the previously-hidden grain.

Most people are happy to complete their first bowl, whatever it looks like, and immediately want to start another, to improve on the shape and the finish of the first.

It's useful to keep your early attempt as a standard to assess future progress. Now and then I come across my first efforts in a cupboard, recall the fight I had to get it finished in a day and muse on how ugly it is.

Every bowl I turn is an attempt to marry the shape to the dimensions of the blank and the character of the grain and get the finish as good as I can.

For your first bowl I suggest you obtain a blank 200mm (8in) in diameter by about 50mm (2in) deep, cut into a circle with the grain running across. Good timbers to use are sycamore, cherry, beech or ash, because they are fairly cheap and easy to turn.

The tools needed are a bowl gouge and round-nosed scraper. If you have an expanding chuck you'll also benefit from having a square-ended scraper for cutting the recess.

Steps to follow

● Carefully examine the blank before you begin, to decide which side will be the top. Look for cracks, discoloured grain or insect damage which you may wish not to see in the finished article and think of the design, so they can be turned off.

Perhaps there's a crack in the edge of one face – that can be the bottom. There may be a grey patch in the middle of one face – that can be turned away when you hollow the bowl. If there are no flaws, think how to show the grain to best advantage.

Set of bowl turning tools. From the top:
6mm (¼in) carver's gouge;
19mm (¾in) half-round scraper;
12mm (½in) square-ended scraper;
9mm (⅜in) bowl gouge.

● Work out the whole process before you start. If you only have a faceplate you will have to use a different sequence of actions to those for a chuck with expanding collets or jaws.

● Design the bowl before starting to turn. This will be limited by the size of the blank and the available mounting devices. In other words, you cannot make a bowl with a base smaller than your faceplate or the smallest jaws on your chuck plus a suitable rim to support the expansion. Take care to design it within your technical capabilities, at least to start with.

● Safety procedures. Make sure the blank is securely mounted and the lathe speed appropriate. Always rotate the blank by hand before starting the lathe, to ensure it will not snag the tool rest. And always wear face protection.

● Learn to adjust the height of the tool rest so you can cut through the centre of the work. This varies according to whether you are using a scraper or a gouge and is affected by your height relative to the lathe.

Gouges are used with the tool rest below centre height and the cutting edge higher than the handle. Scrapers are used with the tool rest higher than for the gouge, so that when the edge is cutting the centre of the work the handle is higher than the edge.

● Teach yourself to use the gouge correctly. While you are learning it's a sound idea to use a gouge with the flute (the channel that runs along the tool) pointing in the direction of cut. Cut with the part of the edge just below the nose, and use the bevel to adjust the depth of cut. If it's nearly rubbing the cut will be shallow, and as you move it further away the depth increases.

● Take account of the effect of grain direction. Bowl blanks are normally cut from planks, so on the lathe the grain runs at right angles to the lathe's axis, in other words the end grain appears on the edge of the blank.

In all woodworking operations it's easier to cut wood with the grain, which produces a cleaner finish from the tool. So it's most efficient to turn the outside of the bowl from the

smaller diameter to the larger and to hollow from the rim to the middle.

● Keep your tools sharp at all times. A blunt tool cuts slowly and leaves a poor finish. It's dangerous because, in order to make it cut, you tend to press too hard and lift the bevel too far off the surface, making a catch more likely.

The process

Having decided which face of the blank will be the top, mount a faceplate in the centre, using four screws which project at least 13mm (½in) into the wood. Screw this onto the lathe and check to see that the mounting is secure. If you can make it wobble on the faceplate take it off the lathe and tighten the screws.

Positioning the tool rest.

Set the lathe speed at about 790rpm and position the tool rest parallel to the bottom of the blank and just below the centre. Hold the gouge on the tool rest and check that the correct part of the cutting edge will be able to cut the centre. Adjust the height accordingly.

Rotate the blank by hand to see that it does not touch the tool rest. Start the lathe to check that the mounting is concentric. If there is a lot of vibration it shows the faceplate was not centred or that the blank is not an accurate circle.

A wobbling blank must not add to the problems beginners face, so it makes sense to remount the bowl or cut it more accurately before starting to turn.

It's possible to turn the side of the blank to make it true, but this is not the easiest cut because the cut is not supported before contact is made with an uneven surface.

When the blank is centred, the next

task is make the bottom clean and slightly concave. You turn the dirty old surface off the bowl to check that no flaws were concealed by grime or saw marks, and make the bottom concave so the bowl will be stable.

Use the bowl gouge for this cut and cut either from the outside to the centre or vice versa. The advantage of cutting from the centre is that you start with the tool resting on solid wood. This is reassuring if you are not sure of the correct angle to hold the tool.

Unfortunately, this direction of cut presupposes that you have easy access to the bottom of the blank, which is the case if you are working on a Union Graduate short-bed lathe or the outboard of many other makes.

But if you work over a bed with the lathe close to the wall you are not so fortunate, and will have to work from the outside towards the centre.

Sure of angle

Once you are sure about the angle to hold the tool, you can do the whole of the bottom in this direction. But until you are sure, start the cut a little way in from the edge.

There's no reason why the whole of the bottom should be flattened, as the edge will be removed when the outside of the bowl is shaped. So long as you can see no flaws in the wood and that the bottom is concave in the middle, you can go on to the next step.

Mark the size of your chuck jaws or faceplate on the bottom. Decide how big the base will be accordingly, and mark with a pencil. If using a chuck, hollow the recess with the gouge and flatten the bottom with a square-ended scraper.

I grind the end of my scraper to the same angle as the jaws on my

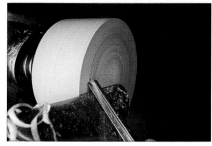
Truing the bottom.

expanding chuck, so that when the end is flat on the bottom of the recess and the side is flush with the walls of the recess, it produces an overhang. Check to see that the chuck fits before going on.

Shape the outside of the bowl with the gouge supported by the flat bottom, working towards the rough sides. Tackle the corners first and with each subsequent cut start nearer the mark, sizing the base and end further up the sides.

To keep control of the cut you have to maintain bevel support, which means that as the tool tip cuts around the curve the end of the handle has to move in the same arc, but by a larger distance because the tool rest acts like a fulcrum.

I tend to leave the outside rough and do a finishing cut after reversing the bowl, in case I need to alter the shape or make it more concentric.

Rounding the side of the bowl.

You may find it easier to get at the outside at this stage, in which case get a really good sharp edge on the gouge and do a delicate finishing cut right across the outside, in one controlled sweep, so little sanding should be needed.

Sand the bottom of the bowl but avoid abrading the wall of the recess, which tends to round over the dovetail. Take the bowl from the lathe and remove the faceplate, putting it back on the bottom of the bowl if that is your only option.

If you have a chuck, put that on the lathe and fit the bowl to it to check that it's concentric, before final tightening.

True up the top

True up the top using a gouge as you did for the bottom. Measure the depth with one ruler across the base and another along the side, and drill a central hole either with straight 6mm (¼in) carver's gouge, ground straight across, or a drill bit in a Jacob's chuck.

Do this to the depth of the bowl minus about 18mm (¾in), so that when the centre disappears in the hollowing process you have a little way to go before reaching the ideal bottom thickness of about 13mm (½in).

Establish the rim thickness of 13mm(½in) with the corner of the square-ended scraper. Using the gouge, hollow out from the centre, making the inside deeper and wider with each cut. Try to mirror the outside shape as you progress.

Using a scraper in the recess.

The flute of the gouge should point up to about 2 o'clock and you should aim to have the bevel fairly flush with the inside to give you control. So the tool handle must start to the right of the centre of the bowl and end up well over to the left by the time the tool reaches the bottom of the hollow.

When the hollowing is nearly complete, gauge the evenness of the wall thickness by finger and thumb, or by callipers when the bowl is stationary. Some parts will need thinning and this is the difficult bit, for you need to be able to remove material exactly where you want. Before doing this, run the gouge around the inside as if you were turning but with the shoulder of the gouge rubbing and the edge a fraction from the surface, and you will feel where the ridges are. This is quite safe because the edge is not in contact to catch.

Repeat process

If you repeat the process but this time when you come across a ridge lift the shoulder off the surface slightly and bring the edge into contact and after it lift off the edge and put the pressure back on the shoulder, you will feather the cut to vary its depth.

When all major rough patches have been removed and the inside is more or less smooth, you may be able to improve the surface by taking a light cut around the inside with the biggest round-nosed scraper you can afford.

The success of this will vary with the wood and delicacy of touch. I sometimes find a scraper roughens the surface, and have to go back to the gouge to get the best finish before sanding.

Sharpening tools is as difficult as using them. The best clue as their sharpness is to see whether any light is reflected from the edge.

Follow the manufacturer's profile when sharpening, until you see the need to change it and have a clear idea as to the shape you want.

Keep the bevel concave by keeping it flush with the rim of your grinder and try to reproduce the lines left by the manufacturer's own grindstone. ∎

Starting to hollow.

The middle of hollowing.

Reaching the centre.

owl turning is fascinating, because unlike other most other branches of woodwork you open up the heart of a lump of wood and see the grain in all its aspects. Spindle turning, on the other hand, is usually seen as more routine, as you only see the outside of the wood and tend to make useful objects. It is, however, more difficult than bowl turning, partly because of the number of tools to master but also because you have to be more precise.

Only rarely do bowls need to conform to strict dimensions, but if you are making table legs it helps if the tenons fit the joints and the lengths are the same. Added to this, if you are a professional you will need to work fast, or your charges will be too high to be commercially viable.

The lathe

Spindles are made between centres on the lathe and are rotated by the driving centre at the headstock end. The dogs on the centre should be kept sharp and should be forced into the end of the work off the lathe by striking the blunt end with a wooden mallet. The tailstock supports the centre at the other end of the wood and this engages in an indentation best made before the blank is mounted.

The tailstock should be put in position so that the centre can go into the end, and fixed on the bed. The centre is moved into the end of the work by rotating the quill and rotated back half a turn before it is locked in place by a nut.

Teaching spindles

When I teach spindle turning I concentrate on four tools with which you can do most things and which introduce you to the basic principles of spindle tool use (photo 1). I also stress that these tools should only be used for spindle turning, because that prevents confusion at a stage where students are having to get to grips with a lot of new information.

Spindle turning needs practice, which is best done on short, straight lengths of unseasoned branches, about 250mm (10in) long and between

Spindle school

Teaching spindle turning to beginners

Set of spindle turning tools (from the top): roughing gouge, spindle gouge, beading and parting tool, and skew chisel.

50mm (2in) and 75mm (3in) in diameter. This is because they are fairly easy to obtain for nothing and being round to start with present less of a challenge than square-section stock.

Green timber is easier to turn than dry wood, and can produce long streamers of shavings, which is encouraging. Most types of wood are suitable, but fruitwoods such as cherry are best, because as well as being easy to turn they have a delightful smell.

Roughing gouge

I introduce the roughing gouge first, because it's what you start with anyway. It is quite easy to sharpen by rolling on the tool rest of the bench grinder and its proper use demonstrates the need to keep the bevel close to the surface of the wood for efficient cutting.

Because the blank is straight, once

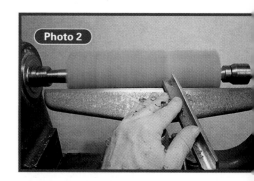

Roughing out a branch with the roughing gouge.

the tool is in the correct position on the work it can only progress along the work cutting with the same efficiency if that angle remains the same (photo 2).

The best way of doing this is if it is held against the body and the body moves by shifting the weight from one foot to the other. It's much harder

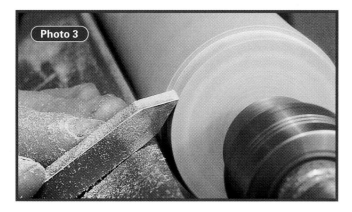

Starting a spigot with the beading and parting tool.

Finishing the spigot with the beading and parting tool.

to try to control the tool by just moving the arms.

Beading and parting tool

The beading and parting tool is a favourite of mine because it is so versatile. The main use of it at this stage is to turn the spigots at each end of the work to provide a safety margin so that if the tool slips off the end of the work it will not hit the driving or tailstock centre.

Teaching its use shows how some tools need to pass over the tool rest as well as along it and you can see that this is because if it did not go up and over then the bevel would not stay in close support (photos 3 and 4).

I know this tool is capable of doing a lot more than bulk removal in skilled hands, but think that for a beginner it's better to teach this function and to

use the spindle gouge and skew for shaping beads and coves.

Some people prefer to use the spindle gouge for shaping and some prefer the skew chisel. As a teacher one has to cover both and allow the student to make a choice. I introduce the gouge first because this is less daunting but I get my students to change the profile by grinding back the sides. This makes it more versatile but it is quite difficult to grind because the tool has to move from side to side and also rotate to keep the bevel the same angle all the way round.

Spindle gouge use

It is used like all gouges, with the flute pointing in the direction of cut and the part of the edge which does the cutting to the right hand side of the nose when cutting from left to right

(photos 5, 6 and 7) and vice versa when cutting to the left.

As with all cutting tools, the bevel should be in close support all the time. To achieve this while turning a bead, the tool needs to be rotated and the handle raised so that at the end of the cut the handle is above the level of the tool rest and over to the side.

A good way to teach this is to get students to move their gouges over a bead before starting the lathe. This means they get to practice without any possibility of having a catch.

Once students have practised one side of a bead, they will have to reverse the action for the other side. It's quite common for this to be a problem.

As a teacher you learn that there are many people who find it easier to move a tool in one direction than

Using a spindle gouge to start a bead.

Halfway through the bead.

At the end of the bead.

Photo 8

Making a cove with the spindle gouge.

another. You have to constantly stress that to move the tool properly for the more difficult side simply requires a reversal of all the actions completed for the easier side. Some people can see this more easily than others.

As a teacher, this is where you have to allow students time and space to practise on their own, while keeping a careful eye open so that major misuses of tools endangering life and limb can be discouraged.

Many students find it hard to remember that the correct part of the edge to use is to the right of the nose when turning to the right, and all you can do as a teacher is constantly remind them. I always try to remember that if they are doing it wrong it is (a) because it is difficult and (b) because I have not taught them yet.

Making a cove

To make a cove, it's easiest to start with a square-sided groove done with the beading and parting tool. If the right hand side of this is rounded like a bead, the bottom of the groove can be rounded by continuing the cut but rotating the gouge so that it finishes in the centre with the flute pointing up (photo 8).

The amount removed should be reduced, as the centre is approached

by pushing the gouge up so that the bevel is rubbing on the work. This has the effect of feathering off the cut so that a ridge is not left in the centre.

Naturally, no attempt should be made to cut up the other side of the groove, as this is working against the grain, a transgression which brings instant punishment in the form of a snag or a rough finish.

If there's time in the course, pupils should be encouraged to practise the use of the gouge by making beads and coves, aiming for consistency of shape and size.

Skew chisel

Anything that can be done with a gouge can be done better with a skew chisel. I teach it by showing how you can use the tool to achieve a smooth finish on a straight cylinder by using it in the planing mode.

It is so much safer, more versatile and easier to use if it is an oval skew ground with a curved edge that I encourage all my pupils to alter their tools before they start. It is easy to change the profile by placing the tool flat on the tool rest of the bench grinder avoiding grinding the point, which needs no modification and should not be rounded.

Making the bevels afterwards is not so easy. Concentrate on making them on each side of the heel, alternating as

you go to keep things even with the edge horizontal.

When you have a sharp edge at the heel, the bevels can be extended to the whole length of the curved edge by rocking the tool on the rest as well as moving it from side to side, it being wider than the wheel. I find it easier to do this by laying my forefinger across the tool rest and holding the tool on to it with my thumb, which acts as a pivot.

Planing cut

The planing cut is done with the point down using the part of the edge, which is near the point (photo 9). The bevel should be close to the surface of the wood but not pressed onto it, which causes ribbing. Rather you should press down onto the tool rest with a slight rotation of the tool in an anti-clockwise direction when cutting from right to left.

The depth of cut is varied by the closeness of the bevel, and the angle of the edge to the axis of the work can be adjusted by small degrees until the most favourable one is found for that piece of wood.

You can use the slicing cut to clean up the sides of a channel made with a parting tool – this leaves a surface which cannot be improved. It's done (photo 10) by taking very thin cuts with the point of the tool, keeping

Photo 9

Using a skew chisel to make a planing cut.

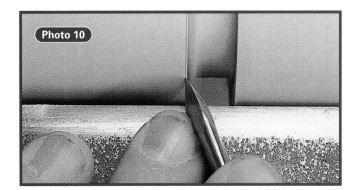

Making a slicing cut with the skew chisel.

The start of a beading cut, made with the skew chisel.

The position of the skew chisel halfway through the beading cut.

The finish of the beading cut made with a skew chisel.

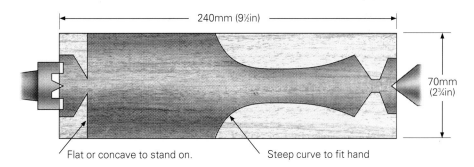

240mm (9½in)

70mm (2¾in)

Flat or concave to stand on.

Steep curve to fit hand

Plan drawing of a simple mallet to make.

the bevel next to the point in close support, but angling the following edge away from the shoulder of the channel as the point goes down. At the end of the cut the point can be lower than the tool rest with the end of the handle higher.

To form a bead with the skew chisel, it's easier to start with a square-sided shoulder formed with a beading and parting tool. The cut is based on the slicing cut but you start with the tool flat on the tool rest and the point a millimetre or two from the shoulder of the bead.

The tool is then rotated (photo 11 and 12) and the handle swung around and up so that the tool finishes with the bevel at right angles to the axis of the work (photo 13). The cut is done completely with the point, which is a lot easier to control than the edge.

Practice is vital with the skew chisel

– about eight hours a day, five days a week for a few years is all it needs. Aim for consistent smooth beads with no random spirals and then you can tackle any job thrown at you.

The first project I give my students is a mallet (see drawing), because it's a simple shape and very useful. It can be made by any combination of the tools so far described, but I prefer to do it mostly with the roughing gouge,

followed by a smoothing cut with the skew. The tools used to make spindles can be used to make objects which have the same grain orientation but involve some hollowing, such as goblets and boxes.

Boxes need precision, because the lid needs to fit well, which takes skill.

I hope that by following next month's article you will be able to make one. ∎

On the box

How to make a simple box

Forming a dovetail spigot.

I enjoy making boxes with well-fitting lids. But I'd been turning for years before I was unable to control my tools precisely enough to make a good one.

The best woods to use are close-grained hardwoods such as boxwood, laburnum, and fruitwoods. But the professional approach to making a new project is to try out the techniques and procedure on cheap timber, so mistakes are inexpensive. You don't even need a good finish on your first attempt, provided you've learnt the process.

Straight-grained

Use a piece of dry, straight-grained timber, because this is easier to work and you stand a better chance of matching the grain in the lid with that in the base.

The example shown here is ash, about 50 x 50 x 125mm (2 x 2 x 5in), with the grain running along the long axis. Boxes are made in this orientation mainly because the lid will stay a better fit if the end grain is in the top, as wood distorts more evenly across the end grain than along the side grain.

Ash is not normally the best timber for boxes because of its open grain and poor stability – but this piece was exceptionally hard and dense.

You will need a chuck of some sort to hold the blank for hollowing the lid and bottom. I used an Axminster four-jaw with dovetail jaws that compress onto a 25mm (1in) spigot, giving a very strong grip.

Many other chucks can do the job, including the cup chuck, which is basically a disc of wood on the faceplate with a tapered hole in the middle.

Turn the blank to a cylinder between centres and form the appropriate spigot on the end for your chuck. The Axminster chuck requires a dovetail-shaped spigot. I make one from a cylindrical spigot of about 30mm (1½in), using a beading and parting tool, and then make the dovetail shape using the left point of the edge (photo 1).

I do this at the tailstock end to avoid catching the driving centre dogs. The tailstock and driving centre are then removed, the chuck installed and the blank inserted.

Adjustable chuck

If you are using an adjustable chuck, clean up the end of the blank to remove the marks left by the driving centre and form a dovetail spigot, so you can part off the lid and mount it in the chuck for hollowing.

This spigot will eventually be a finial on top of the lid. It's useful to get a good finish on the lid's top surface with the point of the skew chisel, using a slicing cut, because the beading tool leaves a rough finish. The top of the lid should be square at this stage, so that it fits snugly on the chuck jaws.

If you are using a cup chuck, it's not a good idea to part off the lid and remove the bottom section from the chuck to mount the lid in the same chuck, as you may have problems remounting the bottom accurately afterwards. You will either have to use the bottom as a temporary cup chuck by making a tapered hole in it the same size as you make the spigot or you will have to make another cup chuck on another faceplate for the lid.

Decide how deep you want the lid, and then add a few millimetres for luck. In my example

Parting off the lid, showing the angle of the tool.

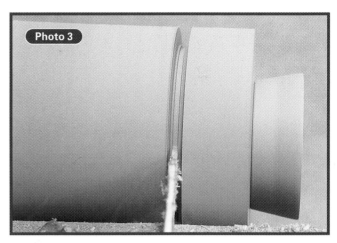

Photo 3

Parting off the lid, leaving steps.

it's about 15mm (⅝in), but it must be in proportion to the bottom and the width.

Now part off the lid. I once did this with a hacksaw, but then read of a better ploy by Chris Stott. You make a groove at the junction as deep as the thickness you want the lid wall to be, plus a few millimetres, using a 4mm (5⁄32in) parting tool and then part off the lid in the centre of this groove using an even narrower parting tool. In photos 2 and 3 I'm using a 1.6mm (1⁄16in) parting tool designed by Chris.

Time saver

This technique leaves steps on both lid and bottom which represent the approximate diameter of the hole to be made in the lid and the lip to be formed on the bottom (photo 4). It saves measuring and, therefore, time.

Mount the lid in the chuck for hollowing. I use a spindle gouge with ground-back sides for this (photo 5). Because you are hollowing into end grain you have to drill a hole, with the gouge, in the centre to the depth required. Don't make the lid too deep, as the top must be thick enough to support the finial.

Remove material from the lid by cutting from the centre hole outward, aiming to hollow nearly up to the step left when parting off the lid.

Get a good finish on the part of the lid that will fit the lip to be formed on the bottom. This must be concave, so that there will be no gap between the lid and bottom. It has to be done with the tool, as sanding will not produce a true surface.

I do this by moving the tool rest to the side and taking a thin cut with the point of the skew. But it can be done with a gouge from the front of the lid. It usually leaves a few fibres

Photo 4

The parted-off lid and bottom.

Photo 5

Hollowing the lid.

Photo 6

Cutting the sides of the lid with a square-ended scraper.

Photo 7

Forming a lip with the beading and parting tool.

waving around inside the lid, which will be removed when truing up the sides of the lid.

These should be parallel or slightly overhung to remain a good fit. It's a major fault to have the sides tapering, because the lid will never be a good fit.

I true up the sides using a 13mm(½in) square-ended scraper, with the left side ground so that the bottom edge does not snag on the sides as the tool goes in (photo 6).

The same tool can be used to smooth the underside of the top, making little steps from the centre outwards with the left corner and then a gentle cut across the face to remove the ridges.

Being end grain, the underside of the top is unforgiving, and if you try to cut too much there will be a catch. I get a very good finish from this tool by sharpening it on my Tormek with a longer bevel than the manufacturer's. I grind the top and bottom surfaces on the side of the wheel to remove any burrs and then hone all surfaces on the leather wheel.

A lick of oil

If you do get a problem with the end grain picking up, a lick of oil or wax should soften the grain and allow a cleaner cut.

You can sand the underside of the lid, but avoid all contact between abrasive and the sides, as this will make the sides uneven, due to differences in the hardness of the grain.

Remove the lid from from the chuck and re-mount the bottom. Using a beading and parting tool (photo 7) form the lip on the bottom. The step left when parting off is a guide to the diameter, but only make a narrow lip at first, so that if you go too far you can remove it and start again without having lost too much wood.

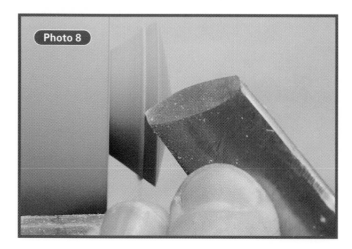

Photo 8

Shaping the finial.

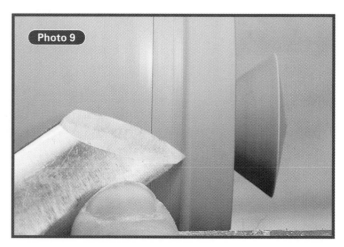

Photo 9

Smoothing the sides with a skew.

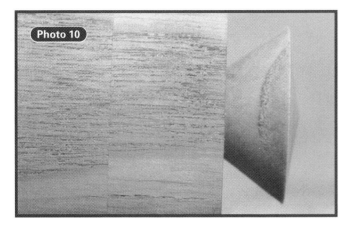

Photo 10

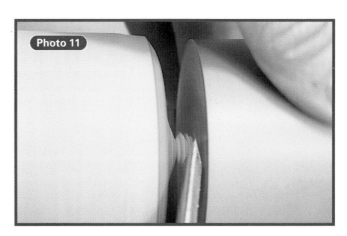

Photo 11

The finish from the skew.

Parting off the bottom.

When the fit is almost achieved, remove the merest slivers with the tool to achieve perfection. This can only be done with a razor-sharp tool.

When the fit is very snug, lengthen the lip and fit the lid. It must be very tight at this stage, because it's likely to slacken when the inside of the box is hollowed, because the heat generated by the tool dries the wood.

With the lid in place, shape the finial (photo 8) and make a finishing cut on the outside with the skew chisel (photo 9). Photo 10 shows the finish from the tool and the grain nearly matching up. Sanding the outside with anything coarser than 320 grit will result in differential abrading, and the lid and bottom will not be flush.

Hollow the inside with a gouge, as in the lid. The sides and bottom can be finished using the square-ended scraper. Again, if you need to do a

finishing cut on the top surface, it's best to do it before your final cut inside, so you can remove any loose fibres that you push in. If necessary, sand the inside.

Replace the lid and check its fit. The final fit should not be ultra-tight, as this makes it hard to remove, particularly when the sides are flush.

If it needs a little loosening, try holding it still as the bottom rotates. Don't be too aggressive, or you may burn it. If it's far too tight, remove a tiny amount with the beading and parting tool, but avoid sanding.

A very tight lid

For a very tight lid, it's a good idea to do a different design. By shaping the top you can make it easier to grip and by accentuating the join with beads, make it easier to insert a fingernail. I use the skew chisel to part, as it enables me to achieve a

good finish, requiring little work to complete the bottom. If you can use the tool one-handed (photo 11) you can support the box with the other hand, but don't grip too hard or a plug may be pulled out of the bottom. I know, because I've done it.

If you are not ready for this level of excitement, use the narrow parting tool and leave enough wood in the bottom to give you room for a finishing cut after you've re-mounted the box.

This can be done on a spigot turned from the stub left in the chuck, but if there isn't enough wood you can mount it on small jaws. But you will need to protect the box with some cloth or tissue. I usually make a couple of passes across the bottom with a sharp skew. Once you've mastered the simple box, there are limitless design possibilities, both functional and aesthetic. ■

Photo 12

The bottom mounted on the spigot.

Photo 13

The completed box.

The right way to make a variety of different boxes

Boxing clever

I like to perfect a new box shape by putting a piece of cheap timber on the lathe and trying out the shape in wood. One of the things to get right is the proportion between the lid and the bottom. I find this is easier to see in 3-D than in a drawing.

It's important to remember that the shape must look good when upright, rather than horizontal as it is on the lathe. The balance is completely different in each of these orientations, which has a profound affect on your perception of the shape.

When an object is horizontal (photo 1) you may find that you want it to balance about a central point, whereas when it's vertical you may prefer it to be bottom heavy so that it

looks stable (photo 2). The effect of light is also important. When I'm turning I have two light sources from above which make the shadows around beads diffuse and the beads look shallow. When a box is in use the light source will normally be from above, casting deep shadows in the grooves, which make them look deeper.

A simple cylindrical shape needs a lot of tool precision, because the use of abrasives on the join between lid and bottom will usually make the two parts slightly oval, so that the join is smooth only in one position.

If you cannot get a good finish from the tool and need to use abrasives, it is best to make the junction between lid and bottom obvious by, for example, adding beads. These can be made with the point of a skew chisel, and you will notice in photo 2 that I have echoed them with a bead around the base to give the design artistic integrity.

You can also shape the top so it is easier to grip. I use this box for throat

sweets, and I carry it in my pocket when I am teaching or singing in a choir.

Tea caddies

Tea caddies have two main design criteria – to be airtight and to hold a standard quantity of tea (125g or 250g). I used to think it would be wise to avoid using a smelly wood, but having used an elm caddy for years with no ill effects, I am changing my advice to exclude resinous woods such as cedar. An overhung bottom section gives the impression that the aroma of the tea will be retained in the caddy.

Most of the hollowing for this design is done with a spindle gouge, but I finish off the overhang with a 25mm (1in) wide round-nosed scraper (photo 3). I have modified this so the body of the tool doesn't scrape the top of the other side of the lip as it goes in. A scraper with an angled insert such as on the Sorby RS 2000 system will also do the trick.

After the practical constraints have been satisfied, aesthetics come into play. I took the unsubtle decision to give an oriental feel to the shape by echoing a pagoda roof for the lid (photo 4).

Photo 3

Scraper for overhang.

Photo 4

**Ash tea caddie,
80 x 120mm (3⅛ x 4¾in).**

Because the box has to hold 125 grammes of tea, it has plenty of scope to warp when there is any change in ambient moisture content. This will alter the fit of the lid. For this reason I use fairly stable timbers such as sycamore or London plane. I rough out the parts in advance, carefully numbering the sections so that they match when they are reunited.

Jewellery box

The yew jewellery box is about 125mm (5in) across and the same in height (photo 5). It has three sections plus a lid (photo 6) and is designed to contain necklaces and earrings.

Because of the size and the relative instability of this timber I roughed out the sections in advance. This releases any tensions locked in the grain, and gives it time to adjust its water content to that of the workshop as opposed to the timber store.

I wanted the grain to match up when the box is closed, so to mount the bIank I used an Axminster four-jaw chuck with Type 'B' jaws which contract onto a 25mm (1in) spigot. I turned a spigot on the end, both to mount the lid for hollowing and to turn into a finial when finishing the box. Then I parted off the lid and remounted it on the same jaws to hollow the inside, leaving wide walls so that any distortion could be turned away.

Having roughed out the inside of the lid I dated it and gave it an identification number so I would be able to match up the parts later. I then remounted the rest of the original blank and hollowed the next section, leaving thick walls again.

This section fits onto the next like a lid, but it had to be remounted onto different jaws that expanded into a 100mm (4in) recess, so I parted it off, marked it and put it aside.

I did the same with the next section and then hollowed the last section with thick walls as before, but leaving it with the spigot on for re-turning later. I then changed the jaws and hollowed the undersides of the middle two sections.

When the sections have had long

Photo 5 **Yew jewellery box closed.**

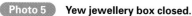

Photo 6

Yew jewellery box open.

enough to warp fully, they can be remounted for finishing off. The inside of the lid can be turned to a finish using the 25mm (1in) spigot jaws to grip on the finial spigot.

The other jaws then need to be used to hold the underside of the next section, so that the inside of its top can be turned and a lip made to support the lid. The lid is then mounted onto the section already on the jaws so that the top surface and finial can be turned to a finish.

As you can see from photo 5, I have accented the joins between the sections with beads because I was unsure that the wood would be stable, and I knew that if there was movement it would show.

My next variation on this design had more definite beads for an even more effective disguise. Although the insides of the sections were finished perfectly, I had to cover them with felt so the necklaces stayed in place when the box was moved.

No matter how hard you try to make the lid fit properly it is very difficult to be sure that the lid will remain tight enough to stay on and yet loose enough to be easily removed.

I discovered one way around this problem in response to one of the oddest commissions I have ever had. The customer wanted a box of a certain timber and a specific size, which is quite usual, but he also said that the lid should be capable of being screwed down so that it could be left in sight but could not be easily

undone by a child. I was told that this had to be done by means of countersunk brass screws.

I knew that if I simply drilled two holes through the lid into the bottom, the hole would quickly loose its thread. I did some research and found you can obtain sets of screws with sleeves that can be inserted into any given material. They are designed for chipboard but work perfectly in wood, provided that the hole is drilled accurately and that you have left enough wall thickness.

I have since made a feature of the screws by making knobs for the top of them (photo 7). These have to be glued in place and are more permanent if the ends of the threads are ground to a chisel end and pushed hard into the knob.

Photo 7 **Olive ash screw-down lid box, 90 x 110mm (3½ x 4¼in).**

Photo 8

Olive ash box open, showing walnut box inside.

Photo 9 **Small boxes.**

This box contains other boxes for keeping items separate (photo 8). It's a good exercise to get the inner boxes to fit so precisely that when they are inserted they slowly descend due to the pressure of air.

Nest of boxes

Like Russian dolls, a nest of boxes serves only to confound the beholder and make them wonder why anyone could be mad enough to want to do such a thing (photo 9).

The trick is to start with the very smallest box you can manage and make sure that the shape is truly cylindrical. The smallest I can manage is 5mm high and 4mm across (³⁄₁₆ x ⁵⁄₃₂in). This needs tools made from masonry nails or any source of tool steel that comes in small enough dimensions.

The main problem with making boxes this small is seeing them while turning. This can be solved by using an embroiderer's combined magnifying glass and lamp. If you drop a component in a pile of shavings, start again!

If you make the next box just big enough to hold the first, and give it very thin walls, you will impress anyone by the number contained in your collection when you get to 37mm (1½in) across.

Soap box

For some purposes, such as holding soap, a box does not need to be picked up to be used, and the lid doesn't need to be a tight fit. In this case the box can be relatively heavy and the lid can fit loosely inside the top of the base on a rim.

There is no great technical skill in doing this because the fit is not precise and the grain does not need to match up. There is, however, great scope for self-expression and for matching the design and timber to suit the decor.

Spillikins box

The biggest difficulty of making boxes in end grain wood is finishing the inside bottom, because any lack of finesse is punished. This problem increases the deeper you get, and when making a box for spillikins (pick-up-sticks) or any other long thin objects, one simple solution is to make the bottom section in two pieces out of the same or contrasting wood. The box in photo 10 has a band of cherry in between the yew segments, made in the same way as the middle section of the jewellery box.

I find that boxes are one of the most satisfying of turning projects because of the challenge to make them perform a specific function while giving endless scope for artistic expression. ■

Photo 10

Spillikins box 40 x 230mm (1⅝ x 9in).

A question of style

How to improve your turning designs, and enter competitions successfully

Woodturning is a great way to pass the time or earn a living. You have a skill to learn, some splendid bits of kit to buy, and you make objects which are unique and all your own work. You can give your work as presents, sell it, or enter competitions.

In all of these instances your work will be examined and judged, according to the perceptions of the person concerned. Your partner will obviously judge it more kindly than a potential buyer.

People at a car boot sale will expect a bargain, while at craft fairs the price you can charge depends on the show's status. In a gallery or shop the public expect to pay a higher price.

Fellow turners look at your work from a different perspective, interested more in technical merit than price.

Making mistakes

As a professional I have been assessed at all these levels. My sternest test came early on, when I submitted pieces for selection to the Devon Guild of Craftsmen. I made a common mistake in choosing the pieces to submit. I didn't find out exactly what the committee was looking for. I chose items which I thought showed a wide range of skills, including turning,

carving and hand-finished work. They wanted evidence of a distinctive style and a sound grasp of one discipline.

Richard Raffan, who was one of the assessors, later told me why I'd failed. He said the candlestick (photo1) was well finished, but the design poor, because the shape didn't look as though it was intended. Some details of the form could have been the results of corrected mistakes, which indeed they were, rather than deliberate design decisions.

To prove yourself as a spindle turner you need to show that you can make two reasonably similar items. At that stage in my career I could not.

My pestle and mortar (photo 2) was a bit rough in places and said to be deficient in its design because the

Photo 2

Elm pestle and mortar.

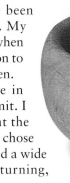

Photo 1

Walnut candlestick

Photo 3

Burr oak bowl.

for the *Woodturning* competition at the Axminster show.

When judging I tend to stress the good points of a piece first. First impressions are important. When assessing work I can tell at once if a piece has 'presence'. If it draws you in to look more closely, then it is more than just a lump of wood someone has hacked into shape.

No formula

There is no mathematical formula for giving this quality, but if you want to ensure the piece is conventionally attractive, make the proportions conform to the 'golden section'. This is the relationship between two dimensions of a rectangle that the Ancient Greeks found to be the most aesthetically pleasing. It can simply be expressed as 1 : 0.6.

This translates to a bowl having a width of 150mm (6in) and a height of 100mm (4in), and multiples thereof. Strangely, pieces with real presence tend to flout convention.

Closer examination reveals whether the promise is justified. For bowls, I look to see if the outside shape is really satisfying. Perhaps the outside shape may look like a continuous curve at first glance, but on closer inspection you find different curves along the surface which indicate a lack of control rather than subtle variations.

sides should have bulged more by about a ¹⁄₁₆ of an inch. At the time I was pleased to be only that much out!

I thought of the criticism as nit picking, but of course Richard was quite right. It's vital to realise that getting the shape correct down to such a degree makes the difference between a good and an ordinary piece.

My burr oak bowl (photo 3) is not a good form. The sides are too straight and the bottom too heavy. The inside was not the same shape as the outside – in other words, the wall thickness was not even.

This advice enabled me to think in more precise design terms. I also realised I would have to put in a lot of practice before I could convince anyone that I was a bowl turner, and even more to become a spindle turner.

Eventually I was selected into the ranks of the Devon Guild and now view other people's work at several different levels. I often have to do a critique of beginners' work in courses I run and am asked for my opinion at woodturning clubs.

At a higher level, I have served on the Devon Guild of Craftsmen's selection committee and was a judge

Photo 4   **Two natural-edge laburnum bowls, the badly shaped one on the right.**

In photo 4, for example, the bowl on the left has a satisfying curve, whereas the one on the right flattens out half-way along. I'd tried to re-turn it after it had warped, and couldn't carry the curve as far as I wanted. Changes of curvature are usually more successful if they are obvious, perhaps punctuated with a bead or cove (photo 5).

For hollow forms like bowls, the inside shape should either correspond or contrast with the outside. If it is neither one or the other this usually indicates a failing in design or execution. I've seen bowls that seemed to have an even wall thickness until I ran my hand down the inside and found a subtle mound which was not intentional.

I am often asked if the bottom of a piece is the right size? This depends on the overall design, but if you can't decide then consult the golden mean. The bottom of a 150 x 100mm (6 x 4in) bowl, for instance, should be 62.5mm (2½in). A wider base would make the bowl look heavier, a smaller base would make it look lighter.

Looks good

Check if the object looks good from all angles. If you are unsure about a shape, remove it from the lathe before finishing and look at it upright on the surface it will sit on.

Try out different shapes with scrap wood. You need not hollow bowls or boxes. Put these items where you will see them every day, and you will eventually decide if you like them.

Decide if the piece is good in terms of what it is made for. Judge a piece on its own merits, not just on whether it fulfils its function but also on whether its maker has been successful. You don't have to like wooden goblets, for instance, to be able to say whether it's a good one.

If you intend to decorate a piece, design the work with this in mind. Decoration, at its best, makes a turned object more 'artistic', so embellishments should add to a piece, not just be tacked on as an after-thought.

Photo 5   Ebonised tea caddy with coves.

Choose the wood carefully for the decoration. If adding surface detail, ask yourself if it will be enhanced by a strong grain pattern showing through, (usually it is not).

On the other hand, curly grain that dries and moves after completion can look wonderful under a black stain. You see the structure of the wood without the distraction of the natural colours. It's important to finish the surface of the piece well before applying decoration, as it usually cannot disguise poor workmanship.

The quality of the finish should be first class, but I place it second to design because although a bad or inappropriate finish will reduce the impact of a good design, an excellent finish will never make a badly-conceived piece into a good one.

The first aspect of finish to be aware of is the removal of torn grain. This is best done with the tool, but if all else fails abrasives should complete the job, provided any modification of

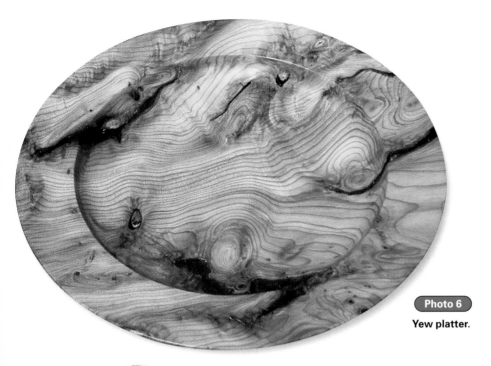

Yew platter.

the shape that results is deliberate. Choose carefully the finish applied to the work. Shiny finishes detract from the impact of work made from spectacularly-grained wood such as burrs, because the surface reflections are visible and impair your view of the grain.

The grain of the yew platter (photos 6 and 7) is easily appreciated because of the matt finish. Dense, fairly featureless woods such as boxwood or beech can be improved by a high-gloss finish.

The finish

The finish you use depends not only on the visual effect wanted, but also on the function of the piece. When I make an item food can come into contact with, I use cooking oil as my finish, followed by a little beeswax, as these are non-toxic. I use Danish oil, tung oil or finishing oil for decorative items, as I can control the glossiness by the number of coats I apply.

Perhaps the biggest challenge for a turner is to enter a competition at a show. As a judge at Axminster, I was privileged to examine many pieces of work closely.

It's always difficult to choose winners and losers, and of course

there can only be a limited number who win, but often many fail on points that could have been easily improved. I'd like to offer some advice:

● Always comply with the category requirements. If you are in any doubt, consult the organisers. A decorated platter is one to which decoration has been applied, not one which is made of a decorative wood such as a burr. A plain bowl should not be made of a burr in my opinion, although that is open to debate, and it should not be embellished by carving.

● Don't let your technical skill prevail over your good taste or common sense. If you make a lace bobbin, ensure it is usable. Early

in my career I made some so thin and complicated that they were useless. I would not judge them favourably now.

● Make the design consistent on the top, bottom and sides of the piece. If you have crisp features on the top of a bowl don't have rounded features beneath. For spindles, I think that less is more, but if you add beads and coves use a limited set of styles so the whole piece has a theme.

● Show you have taken the bottom of the piece into consideration in your design. Don't leave the chuck recess unless the shape is part of the design. If you leave screw-holes make sure they are filled well and are not obtrusive.

Evidence of mounting

Evidence of how a piece was mounted on the lathe should not necessarily be removed, certainly not simply to show that you can do it. To remove them or not should be a design decision.

There are many sources of design inspiration, such as exhibitions of craft work, museums, and books like *Wonders in Wood* published by the Association of Woodturners of Great Britain. The way to use these resources is to examine each piece in detail, and develop a critical approach.

Allow yourself to become sensitive to the feelings evoked by the piece, and try to work out why you do or don't like it. This will help you emulate the qualities you admire in others. ■

Close up of yew platter showing grain.

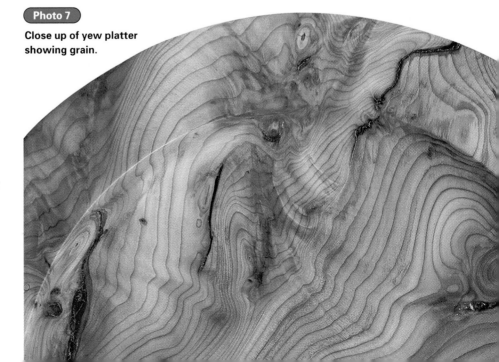

A question of style

Part Two

Some final thoughts on successful design

Ash blank, heart near top.

In my last article I gave my thoughts on design, focusing on competitions and selection committees. But this is not the most common reason to design a turning.

Most design comes from a response to one of two questions – how do I turn this lump of wood into something beautiful? And, how do I make a functional object work effectively? Both questions need a different approach.

The first question crops up when a beginner is given a faceplate blank as a present, or when they have fallen in love with it at a suppliers. If the piece is a spindle blank, it is likely to be either a box or a spindle, so the approach will have more to do with its function.

Before deciding what to make with a piece of wood, it's helpful to know the species and its

properties. Look in your local library for a book on the characteristics of wood.

These books will give you the physical properties of an average sample of the wood, and may include a few words on the traditional uses. The information given often won't contain specific turning recommendations, so use your common sense when interpreting it.

For example, if a wood such as cedar (*Cedrela odorata*), is described as 'coarse and open grained', don't turn it into a thin-walled bowl because it won't be strong enough. Go for a chunky design. If it's a wood prone to decay when exposed to the elements, like sycamore, don't make an outdoor object.

The quality of your sample is as important as the characteristics of the species. Look for any defects you find unattractive and want to exclude from the finished item.

It helps you understand how far a knot or crack will go by working out the position the blank occupied on the tree. Look for long grain, which runs along the length of the tree; this shows the orientation of the blank. If the long grain is on the flat of a circular blank (see photos), end grain will appear in two places on the sides.

If the end grain is in the form of semi-circular rings (photo 1) the blank was cut from near the heart. The heart would have been near the flat, which is nearest the centre of the semi-circles (the top in photo 1), and the sapwood is on the bottom.

If the end grain runs vertically from top to bottom, the blank was cut a long way from the heart, on the quarter, and it may be difficult to say where the heart lay. This sort of blank is the most stable because there is little tension in the wood.

Usually the grain is between these two extremes, and you can see the end grain is curved to some extent. Photo 2 is of typical ash, the colouration showing that the heart was towards the bottom left.

Ash blank cut nearly on the quarter.

Photo 3

Cedar blank with knot.

Having worked out the orientation you will be able to understand the extent of any defects. There may be a patch of grey or yellow wood indicating the first stage of rot. Often this will be in the sapwood, so you may be able to design your bowl so it is near the bottom and can be turned away.

The same applies to shakes. Even experienced turners have trouble predicting the extent of these. Cracks in the end grain may extend a long way into the wood, and be difficult to turn through, whereas cracks running parallel to the grain where the heart is, with both ends visible, should be more predictable.

Knots are another matter. To understand them you need to remember they represent the traces of old branches. Many people find them attractive, particularly when the grain curls around a knot in waves, described as 'ripple'.

But they are another centre of stress, which can cause instability in the finished item. In other words, cracks may grow from them after the piece is finished. You can sometimes predict the extent and nature of a knot by reading the blank. If the knot appears on two surfaces (photo 3) it obviously extends through the whole blank.

I turned a cedar blank into a bowl (photo 4). The knot wasn't attractive and I wanted to lose it, so I made the top overhang and all that remains of it is the light coloured area on the side.

Because cedar is fairly soft I rounded the rim inside. This is less likely to be damaged than a sharp rim,

but I made it look crisp by putting a groove on the inside. The shape would have worked as a continuous, smooth curve, but I added interest to a fairly bland wood by adding a bead. The curve of the wall extends under the bead, while the surface of the bead complements the curve of the wall.

The deep grooves above and below the bead accentuate it, making it look more definite. I removed all traces of the mounting recess because I wanted it to be a continuous curve underneath (photo 5).

If you can't remove a knot, make it into a feature. Whether you eventually fill it or not is up to you. I favour filling if the bowl is to be used for food, as a knot can harbour germs if food particles lodge inside.

My preferred filling is wood dust and superglue. I pour the glue inside and add the dust. If the dust is not all set by the glue, I pour more onto it, adding dust and glue until the hole is well filled.

Sanding dust is best, as it is fine. I like to use dust from the wood I am turning so it blends in, but some prefer a contrasting colour. If you need it to be dark for contrast, or because the knot is darker than the wood, use bark dust. Hold the bark against a rotating sanding disc, with an empty tin to catch the dust.

The smell of superglue irritates my nose and, whenever possible, I use it in a well-ventilated area, as recommended on most containers.

If the knot appears on only one

Photo 4

Cedar bowl
275 x 75mm (11 x 3in).

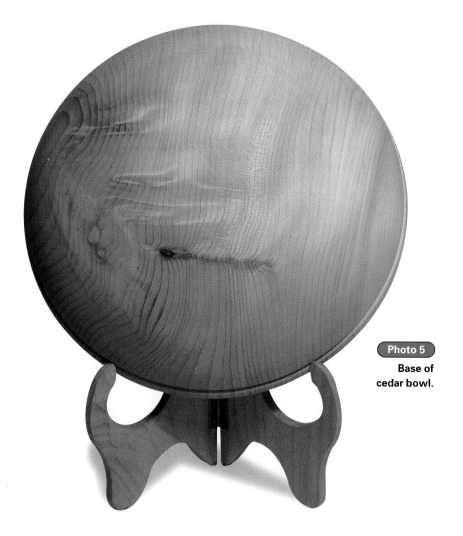

Photo 5

Base of
cedar bowl.

grain or colour is interesting, exploit it by the form you choose.

In a wood like ash you may get a nice brown colour in the heart which only appears on one side of the face (photo 10). I like to include it in the top of the piece. If I'm making a rim I may make it just as wide as the colouration to make the most of it.

Also, if there is a particularly nice figure inside the bowl, it would be a shame to make a closed form which prevents you from seeing it.

The moisture content of the timber is important in turning terms, but is not strictly a design consideration. It's safer to presume it is not in equilibrium with your ambient humidity and, where possible, should be roughed out and allowed to dry before it is finished.

Blanks up to 50mm (2in) thick can be dried by storing them in a dry area such as a cupboard with a dehumidifier inside, provided that the sides of the blank are sealed with emulsified paraffin wax (end-grain sealer), PVA glue, or old spirit-based paint.

In photo 7, the blank was put in a kiln on February 10, this year, and although it was down to 12% moisture content when turned, it distorted afterwards because of the convoluted grain.

face, it will disappear somewhere in the middle of the blank. Insert a piece of wire to see how deep any fissure goes.

Dead knots are where a branch has grown out of the tree, been cut off, and grown over by the tree. These can disappear a short distance below the surface. Equally, they can appear in the middle of an apparently perfect blank.

This is one of the joys of working with a natural material. The knot in photos 6 and 7 disappeared when rounding the base of the platter I made from it (photos 8 and 9).

Check the colour and patterns of the grain. If the colour is bland and the grain indistinct, your form has to be perfect to be visually interesting, or you can see it as something to colour or carve. If the

Photo 7

Same blank showing
convoluted grain.

Photo 6

Ash platter blank 250 x 32mm (10 x 1¼in) with knot on bottom edge.

Photo 8 — Ash platter.

Photo 9 — Base of ash platter.

Having got to know the blank and decided what you want to do with it, it's a good idea to draw a profile on a sheet of paper. This saves you the frustration of having a shape in your head which cannot be reproduced by the dimensions of your blank.

Start with the profile of your blank, which you can usually draw life size. For very large blanks you may have to draw to scale.

Think through the process you will be following so your design takes into account things like the size of faceplate or chuck, and the depth of screws.

Within the scope of your mounting system, your blank size, and any defects you wish to remove, you can sketch in the shape you want to aim for, bearing in mind the characteristics of the timber.

You only need to draw half of the profile, as you can use a mirror on the halfway point to show the whole shape, or cut out a half profile and draw around it for the other half.

Bear in mind your level of ability when designing. Go for a simple shape at first, and experiment with more difficult profiles as your skills increase.

When you are happy with your design, try to make it. I never have fixed ideas about what I am going to do with a piece, because I like to respond to the wood.

Designing for a purpose

The design process can best be illustrated by a simple project such as a platter (photos 8 and 9). Although platters are functional, they can be used for different things, all of which have to be taken into account when designing them.

My standard range includes two types. The wide-rimmed platter is made of 37mm (1½in) thick timber, of which the 300mm (12in) diameter is the most useful for general-purpose troughing, being deep enough for gravy and even being useful for fruit. The other kind is made of 31mm (1¼in) timber and has a narrow rim. It is specially designed for holding

sandwiches, and can also be used as a tray. Both these platters should be made of stable timber, as they must be flat to prevent rocking. If the grain is as wild as in photo 8, the platter will mainly be an aesthetic object.

You should be able to pick up a platter easily, so it should not have a bottom edge flush with the table. The top rim should not be really thin as it will probably be used often, washed and left to dry on a draining rack, which could damage it.

The most suitable timbers for platters are ash, sycamore, London plane and oak. Cherry looks good but is less durable, and prone to warping and insect attack.

Use timber from a large tree to get a blank which doesn't include the heart, so is less likely to warp. Ideally, the timber should be cut on the quarter, but this tends to be expensive because it is a wasteful way of planking.

I like to make a shallow groove in a wide rim because it makes the grain look good, and you can use it to put cherry stones in. I do not always remove the mounting recess, but if the piece is beautifully figured I take more care, and you can see the curve of the recess matches the curve of the groove in the rim.

More complex items, such as practical household objects, will be discussed in my new series of articles, where the whole design process will be covered in each project. ∎

Photo 10

Ash blank with colouration best used on the rim.

Note

Every effort has been made to ensure that the information in this book is accurate at the time of writing but inevitably prices, specifications, and availability of tools will change from time to time. Readers are therefore urged to contact manufacturers or suppliers for up-to-date information before ordering tools.

Measurements

Throughout the book instances may be found where a metric measurement has fractionally varying imperial equivalents, usually within ¹⁄₁₆in either way. This is because in each particular case the closest imperial equivalent has been given. A mixture of metric and imperial measurements should never be used – always use either one or the other.

See also detailed metric/imperial conversion charts on page 123.

Metric/Imperial Conversion Chart

mm	inch	mm	inch	mm	inch	mm	inch
1	0.03937	27	1.06299	80	3.14960	340	13.38582
2	0.07874	28	1.10236	90	3.54330	350	13.77952
3	0.11811	29	1.14173	100	3.93700		
4	0.15748	30	1.18110			360	14.17322
5	0.19685			110	4.33070	370	14.56692
		31	1.22047	120	4.72440	380	14.96063
6	0.23622	32	1.25984	130	5.11811	390	15.35433
7	0.27559	33	1.29921	140	5.51181	400	15.74803
8	0.31496	34	1.33858	150	5.90551		
9	0.35433	35	1.37795			410	16.14173
10	0.39370			160	6.29921	420	16.53543
		36	1.41732	170	6.69291	430	16.92913
11	0.43307	37	1.45669	180	7.08661	440	17.32283
12	0.47244	38	1.49606	190	7.48031	450	17.71653
13	0.51181	39	1.53543	200	7.87401		
14	0.55118	40	1.57480			460	18.11023
15	0.59055			210	8.26771	470	18.50393
		41	1.61417	220	8.66141	480	18.89763
16	0.62992	42	1.65354	230	9.05511	490	19.29133
17	0.66929	43	1.69291	240	9.44881	500	19.68504
18	0.70866	44	1.73228	250	9.84252		
19	0.74803	45	1.77165				
20	0.78740			260	10.23622		
		46	1.81102	270	10.62992		
21	0.82677	47	1.85039	280	11.02362		
22	0.86614	48	1.88976	290	11.41732		
23	0.90551	49	1.92913	300	11.81102		
24	0.94488	50	1.96850	310	12.20472		
25	0.98425	60	2.36220	320	12.59842		
26	1.02362	70	2.75590	330	12.99212		

1 mm = 0.03937 inch
1 cm = 0.3937 inch
1 m = 3.281 feet
1 inch = 25.4 mm
1 foot = 304.8 mm
1 yard = 914.4 mm

Imperial/Metric Conversion Chart

inch		mm	inch		mm	inch		mm
0	0	0	23/64	0.359375	9.1281	45/64	0.703125	17.8594
1/64	0.015625	0.3969				23/32	0.71875	18.2562
1/32	0.03125	0.7938	3/8	0.375	9.5250	47/64	0.734375	18.6531
3/64	0.046875	1.1906	25/64	0.390625	9.9219			
1/16	0.0625	1.5875	13/32	0.40625	10.3188	3/4	0.750	19.0500
			27/64	0.421875	10.7156			
5/64	0.078125	1.9844				49/64	0.765625	19.4469
3/32	0.09375	2.3812	7/16	0.4375	11.1125	25/32	0.78125	19.8438
7/64	0.109375	2.7781	29/64	0.453125	11.5094	51/64	0.796875	20.2406
			15/32	0.46875	11.9062	13/16	0.8125	20.6375
1/8	0.125	3.1750	31/64	0.484375	12.3031			
9/64	0.140625	3.5719				53/64	0.828125	21.0344
5/32	0.15625	3.9688	1/2	0.500	12.700	27/32	0.84375	21.4312
11/64	0.171875	4.3656	33/64	0.515625	13.0969	55/64	0.858375	21.8281
			17/32	0.53125	13.4938			
3/16	0.1875	4.7625	35/64	0.546875	13.8906	7/8	0.875	22.2250
13/64	0.203125	5.1594	9/16	0.5625	14.2875	57/64	0.890625	22.6219
7/32	0.21875	5.5562				29/32	0.90625	23.0188
15/64	0.234375	5.9531	37/64	0.578125	14.6844	59/64	0.921875	23.4156
1/4	0.250	6.3500	19/32	0.59375	15.0812			
			39/64	0.609375	15.4781	15/16	0.9375	23.8125
17/64	0.265625	6.7469				61/64	0.953125	24.2094
9/32	0.28125	7.1438	5/8	0.625	15.8750	31/32	0.96875	24.6062
19/64	0.296875	7.5406	41/64	0.640625	16.2719	63/64	0.984375	25.0031
5/16	0.3125	7.9375	21/32	0.65625	16.6688			
			43/64	0.671875	17.0656			
21/64	0.1328125	8.3344						
11/32	0.34375	8.7312	11/16	0.6875	17.4625	1 inch = 1.000 = 25.40 mm		

Index

WOODCARVING

The Art of the Woodcarver	*GMC Publications*
Carving Birds & Beasts	*GMC Publications*
Carving Nature: Wildlife Studies in Wood	*Frank Fox-Wilson*
Carving on Turning	*Chris Pye*
Carving Realistic Birds	*David Tippey*
Decorative Woodcarving	*Jeremy Williams*
Elements of Woodcarving	*Chris Pye*
Essential Tips for Woodcarvers	*GMC Publications*
Essential Woodcarving Techniques	*Dick Onians*
Further Useful Tips for Woodcarvers	*GMC Publications*
Lettercarving in Wood: A Practical Course	*Chris Pye*
Power Tools for Woodcarving	*David Tippey*
Practical Tips for Turners & Carvers	*GMC Publications*
Relief Carving in Wood: A Practical Introduction	*Chris Pye*
Understanding Woodcarving	*GMC Publications*
Understanding Woodcarving in the Round	*GMC Publications*
Useful Techniques for Woodcarvers	*GMC Publications*
Wildfowl Carving – Volume 1	*Jim Pearce*
Wildfowl Carving – Volume 2	*Jim Pearce*
The Woodcarvers	*GMC Publications*
Woodcarving: A Complete Course	*Ron Butterfield*
Woodcarving: A Foundation Course	*Zoë Gertner*
Woodcarving for Beginners	*GMC Publications*
Woodcarving Tools & Equipment Test Reports	*GMC Publications*
Woodcarving Tools, Materials & Equipment	*Chris Pye*

WOODTURNING

Adventures in Woodturning	*David Springett*
Bert Marsh: Woodturner	*Bert Marsh*
Bill Jones' Notes from the Turning Shop	*Bill Jones*
Bill Jones' Further Notes from the Turning Shop	*Bill Jones*
Bowl Turning Techniques Masterclass	*Tony Boase*
Colouring Techniques for Woodturners	*Jan Sanders*
The Craftsman Woodturner	*Peter Child*
Decorative Techniques for Woodturners	*Hilary Bowen*
Faceplate Turning	*GMC Publications*
Fun at the Lathe	*R.C. Bell*
Further Useful Tips for Woodturners	*GMC Publications*
Illustrated Woodturning Techniques	*John Hunnex*
Intermediate Woodturning Projects	*GMC Publications*
Keith Rowley's Woodturning Projects	*Keith Rowley*
Multi-Centre Woodturning	*Ray Hopper*
Practical Tips for Turners & Carvers	*GMC Publications*
Spindle Turning	*GMC Publications*
Turning Green Wood	*Michael O'Donnell*
Turning Miniatures in Wood	*John Sainsbury*
Turning Pens and Pencils	*Kip Christensen & Rex Burningham*
Turning Wooden Toys	*Terry Lawrence*
Understanding Woodturning	*Ann & Bob Phillips*
Useful Techniques for Woodturners	*GMC Publications*

Useful Woodturning Projects	*GMC Publications*
Woodturning: Bowls, Platters, Hollow Forms, Vases, Vessels, Bottles, Flasks, Tankards, Plates	*GMC Publications*
Woodturning: A Foundation Course (New Edition)	*Keith Rowley*
Woodturning: A Fresh Approach	*Robert Chapman*
Woodturning: An Individual Approach	*Dave Regester*
Woodturning: A Source Book of Shapes	*John Hunnex*
Woodturning Jewellery	*Hilary Bowen*
Woodturning Masterclass	*Tony Boase*
Woodturning Techniques	*GMC Publications*
Woodturning Tools & Equipment Test Reports	*GMC Publications*
Woodturning Wizardry	*David Springett*

WOODWORKING

Bird Boxes and Feeders for the Garden	*Dave Mackenzie*
Complete Woodfinishing	*Ian Hosker*
David Charlesworth's Furniture-Making Techniques	*David Charlesworth*
Furniture & Cabinetmaking Projects	*GMC Publications*
Furniture-Making Projects for the Wood Craftsman	*GMC Publications*
Furniture-Making Techniques for the Wood Craftsman	*GMC Publications*
Furniture Projects	*Rod Wales*
Furniture Restoration (Practical Crafts)	*Kevin Jan Bonner*
Furniture Restoration and Repair for Beginners	*Kevin Jan Bonner*
Furniture Restoration Workshop	*Kevin Jan Bonner*
Green Woodwork	*Mike Abbott*
Making & Modifying Woodworking Tools	*Jim Kingshott*
Making Chairs and Tables	*GMC Publications*
Making Classic English Furniture	*Paul Richardson*
Making Fine Furniture	*Tom Darby*
Making Little Boxes from Wood	*John Bennett*
Making Shaker Furniture	*Barry Jackson*
Making Woodwork Aids and Devices	*Robert Wearing*
Minidrill: Fifteen Projects	*John Everett*
Pine Furniture Projects for the Home	*Dave Mackenzie*
Router Magic: Jigs, Fixtures and Tricks to Unleash your Router's Full Potential	*Bill Hylton*
Routing for Beginners	*Anthony Bailey*
The Scrollsaw: Twenty Projects	*John Everett*
Sharpening: The Complete Guide	*Jim Kingshott*
Sharpening Pocket Reference Book	*Jim Kingshott*
Space-Saving Furniture Projects	*Dave Mackenzie*
Stickmaking: A Complete Course	*Andrew Jones & Clive George*
Stickmaking Handbook	*Andrew Jones & Clive George*
Test Reports: *The Router* and *Furniture & Cabinetmaking*	*GMC Publications*
Veneering: A Complete Course	*Ian Hosker*
Woodfinishing Handbook (Practical Crafts)	*Ian Hosker*
Woodworking with the Router: Professional Router Techniques any Woodworker can Use	*Bill Hylton & Fred Matlack*
The Workshop	*Jim Kingshott*

VIDEOS

Drop-in and Pinstuffed Seats	*David James*	Twists and Advanced Turning	*Dennis White*
Stuffover Upholstery	*David James*	Sharpening the Professional Way	*Jim Kingshott*
Elliptical Turning	*David Springett*	Sharpening Turning & Carving Tools	*Jim Kingshott*
Woodturning Wizardry	*David Springett*	Bowl Turning	*John Jordan*
Turning Between Centres: The Basics	*Dennis White*	Hollow Turning	*John Jordan*
Turning Bowls	*Dennis White*	Woodturning: A Foundation Course	*Keith Rowley*
Boxes, Goblets and Screw Threads	*Dennis White*	Carving a Figure: The Female Form	*Ray Gonzalez*
Novelties and Projects	*Dennis White*	The Router: A Beginner's Guide	*Alan Goodsell*
Classic Profiles	*Dennis White*	The Scroll Saw: A Beginner's Guide	*John Burke*

MAGAZINES

WOODTURNING ✦ WOODCARVING FURNITURE & CABINETMAKING
THE DOLLS' HOUSE MAGAZINE
THE ROUTER ✦ THE SCROLLSAW BUSINESSMATTERS ✦ WATER GARDENING

The above represents a full list of all titles currently published or scheduled to be published.
All are available direct from the Publishers or through bookshops, newsagents and specialist retailers.
To place an order, or to obtain a complete catalogue, contact:

GMC Publications,
Castle Place, 166 High Street, Lewes, East Sussex BN7 1XU, United Kingdom
Tel: 01273 488005 Fax: 01273 478606

Orders by credit card are accepted